"We'll Cooperate."

"How can I begin anything new with all of yesterday in me?" — Leonard Cohen, Beautiful Losers

On January 1st, 1997, John Ramsey was in Atlanta, sitting down for an interview on *CNN*.[1] His wife Patsy was beside him. The host, Brian Cabell, asked the grieving father from Colorado:

CABELL: *When you return to Boulder, you will sit down with the Boulder police?*

JOHN [Nods, then shakes his head]: *Oh, absolutely. Absolutely. We want them to know every-thing possible…[trails off].*

PATSY: *Everything.*

JOHN: *That could help them.*

PATSY: *Whatever they want [head bouncing], whatever anyone wants, we will co-operate.*

Three years and two months later, on March 27th, 2000, the Ramseys were back on *CNN*, toting their new book *The Death of Innocence* in a two-part interview [over two days] on <u>Larry King Live</u>. Larry's first question to the Ramseys was on something he described as "directly current"; the question of a polygraph test.[2] More than three years after JonBenét's death, the Ramseys still hadn't taken one.

Just ten days earlier on Barbara Walters' show, John made the dubious claim that the cops had never actually asked them to take a lie detector test. Walters had seized on this whopper, and asked the couple if they would take a polygraph now. Both said they would. It was a strange situation all-round. While the Ramseys were promoting their book in the media, the same media giving them airplay and PR was asking them about taking a lie detector test.

But now it was Larry's turn to hammer the Ramseys on the same point. So when he opened his show, he opened on precisely this point.

LARRY: *Will you do it [take a polygraph]?*

JOHN: *We have – we were asked, 'Had we been asked to take a lie detector test?' We said, 'No.' We were asked, 'Would we?' We said, 'Certainly we would.' We would expect it to be fair, and we would expect the results to be public.*

That's a lot of verbal diarrhoea instead of a simple yes or no. A month later, the <u>*Washington Post*[3]</u> reported on the Ramseys refusing to take a polygraph. A month after that, on May 25th, 2000, <u>Boulder's *Daily Camera*</u> <u>finally published the results of the tests.</u> The Ramseys said the tests proved they didn't kill their daughter. Beckner said the tests had no value.

Ironically, there wasn't one polygraph test but two. The result of the first[4] was deemed "inconclusive." The Ramseys' attorney Lin Wood, and several experts Wood brought forward to comment publicly on the results, were asked by the media to explain the outcome of the first test. They couldn't.[5]

The Last Photo and what it Means

"I really wish we would stop playing games."
— Patsy Ramsey, May 25th, 2000

On April 13th, 2019, more than 23 years after JonBenét's murder, a brand new "last photo" was released to the media for the first time. Just as the polygraph concession coincided with a little give-and-take between the Ramseys and the media in 2000, it seems the "last photo" in 2019 was a gift in exchange for airplay.

The not-so-good-for-the-Ramseys settlement with *CBS* after the triumphant bluster that foreshadowed it [a $750 million lawsuit filed on behalf of Burke Ramsey, settled, apparently for not a single penny] was meant to be drowned out by a new and contrived deluge. *A&E's* Hunting JonBenét's Killer, and the new "last photo" achieved just that.

What was so special about April 2019 that warranted John Ramsey stepping in front of the cameras, and a poster-sized mock-up of the Ransom Note, and the release of never-before-seen photos? Well, April 2019 was three months after the embarrassing settlement. There were no new clues in the phantasmal hunt for intruders, this was about reputation management, and control of the narrative.

But there are new and real clues lurking in the ether of the new last photo. Unacknowledged, of course. One doesn't need to be a Rocket Scientist to connect the brown, black and white bow in the new last photo to the <u>previously invisible</u> – or <u>obscure</u>, or simply unseen – <u>material peeking out between blonde hairs and curled</u>, but lifeless little-girl's hands. But one does require more than a passing knowledge of the unreleased discovery to know the significance of the bow. And one needs a relatively decent knowledge of the family dynamics to know, beyond the shallow forensic significance, that fact that it's there – what it *means*.

So let's find out. We'll peel back three contextual layers, one at a time, and in so doing, expose a brand new breakthrough in this case.

<u>Worth playing for?</u>

Layer #1

The first layer is the context of this image, and its priority, given that the Ramsey case is the Mount Everest of high-profile criminal cases. Without doubt, the Ramsey case is the most famous American case, and arguably the most famous American case in the rest of the world.

On the comprehensive but not necessarily accurate[6] *PBWorks En-cyclopaedia page on JonBenét Ramsey*, a staggering 76 <u>books have been written</u> [including two books by the Ramseys themselves],[7] <u>approximately 23 documentaries have been released</u> [at an average of one per year for 23 years] and <u>at least three movies</u>. The number of articles in the mainstream media, and <u>appearances related to JonBenét Ramsey</u> in <u>broadcast media</u>, are too many to list, but are in the hundreds, respectively. As of September 2018, the Ramsey case file was said to exceed 60 000 pages. Compare that to the relatively trim 1960 pages of the Watts case.

Now, within this context, of countless books, documentaries and new coverage, think about the effort it had to take to withhold the last photo of JonBenét Ramsey for 23 years. Not only is the last photo crucially important, it's basically the flag fluttering at the top of the Mount

Everest case file. It's where JonBenét's story ends. And yet, instead of providing this image right in the beginning, other images have been used in the various books. The Ramseys have used images from Christmases past in their books, and John Douglas has used images of the Ramseys from as far back as the Christmas of 1994 in his book *Law & Disorder*.

It's no exaggeration to say that this final image of JonBenét – not smiling, isolated, with no one else in the image but her – is perhaps most important image in the entire archive. It's the equivalent of a summit photo of Mount Everest, missing from the expedition. It throws the entire expedition in doubt.

Layer #2

The second layer is the more obvious one – the release of the last photo shortly after the settlement to redirect indignation around the Ramseys to something else besides the Ramseys, and Burke. I found the timing of the settlement to be interesting. The lawsuit remained in effect until early January 2019, allowing a media silence to assert itself right through December and the Christmas of 2018 – arguably for the first time since Christmas 1996 – as media agencies bit their nails waiting to see how the *CBS* thing would be flushed down the drain.

What the Ramseys had succeeded in doing was nipping an unfriendly documentary series in the bud – literally. *CBS* had originally made a six-hour series of three episodes and the third episode, building up to and eventually featuring Burke Ramsey, was never allowed to air. To date it still hasn't. History has subsequently been rewritten to show that it never existed in the first place.

But episode two, the middle child effectively in the trilogy of episodes, was aired just prior to the pulling of the plug on episode three. A few excerpts of episode two are, I think, in order:

"It's not a foreign faction who committed this crime." – <u>Jim Fitzgerald</u>, forensic linguist, appeared on *CBS* episode 2

"I believe this is an inside-of-the-house killing." – <u>Werner Spitz</u>, forensic pathologist, appeared on *CBS* episode 2

"So I think you can eliminate the outside…intruder…hypothesis. So more likely, it's a cover up something. What to cover up?" – <u>Dr. Henry Lee</u>, forensic scientist, appeared on *CBS* episode 2

After being <u>snubbed by Alex Hunter</u> on the phone, the hosts interview Lisa Polansky, a Colorado defense attorney, reading aloud and verbatim the Grand Jury charges against John and Patsy. <u>They refer to one of JonBenét's parents</u> unlawfully, knowingly, recklessly and feloniously allowing JonBenét to be placed in a situation which posed a threat of injury to her life or health, which resulted in the death of Jon-Benét Ramsey, a child under the age of sixteen. The charge was summarized as:

COUNT IV(a) CHILD ABUSE RESULTING IN DEATH.

The other count referred to rendering assistance to a person, with the intention of hindering, delaying, preventing the discovery, detention, apprehension, prosecution, conviction and punishment of some unnamed third party. This unnamed third party, the indictment reads, refers to a mysterious third party suspected of the crime of murder in the first degree.

Having read them, Polansky is asked how come both John and Patsy are referred to as accessories, and yet neither is accused directly of murdering their child. What does this mean?

"Normally, if they do an accessory charge, which here is generally after the fact, it's usually somebody else. My opinion would be that there's a third person…" – <u>Lisa Polansky</u>, Colorado defense attorney, appeared on *CBS* episode 2

"The only person that's left is Burke Ramsey." – Jim Clemente, former New York State prosecutor, former FBI profiler, hosted *CBS* episode 2

When the third person referenced in episode is mentioned, the image used of the Ramseys spending Christmas together – including Burke – is from 1993. This image. Why not any of these? The answer is if John took photos of his family, then he holds the copyright, and wouldn't license it to anyone – whether a documentarian or journalist – who took a hostile approach to the Ramsey's alleged innocence. Obviously in any image in which John himself appears, someone else took the photo and has copyright, and has probably sold it on and licensed it. It's interesting that the best images of JonBenét, and those closest to the time of her death, all belong to the Ramseys, and yet they're only licensed to the "right" authors and media. This gives these handpicked commentators not only access, but better quality material to work with, which makes their storytelling more compelling.

The use of the last photo is the same thing in a long line of carrots. The only difference is, the last photo carrot is something like climbing Mount Everest and waiting 23 years to show that you did. In an authentic scenario [which this case obviously isn't] the last photo ought to have been one of the first and earliest photos released, just as when anyone returns from Mount Everest, the summit photo is purposefully distributed as widely as possible.

The Colorado defense attorney also asserts that even if Burke was involved, legally *Colorado law doesn't recognize murder if the perpetrator is under ten years of old.* Burke was nine years and eleven months. His friend Doug Stine was a similar age as well. The idiosyncrasy of the Ramsey case is that while the law may protect Burke [assuming he was involved], and in so doing render a crime technically not a crime, or technically unprosecutable, if the Ramseys covered up the crime then they as adults could be guilty of being accessories to a murder which – technically – never happened.

Whether you accede to or reject the legal merits, the fact is JonBenét *was* murdered. Besides that she was also tortured, and it appears – and it's certainly the view of True Crime Rocket Science – that she was molested for a length of time. It's unknown whether the dropped 911 call on December 23rd had anything to do with that, but what is certain, is JonBenét was not psychologically healthy or sleeping well or safe in the weeks and days leading up to the Christmas of 1996. The Grand Jury believed she was neglected in such a reckless manner it amounted to child abuse. Child abuse resulting in death.

Curiously, on the official Wikipedia page of the controversial *CBS* series, there is no mention whatsoever of the third episode, nor is there an explicit subheading highlighting the legal proceedings or controversy surrounding the series.[8] What there is is 1) a section emphasizing the "hazy" assertions of the team of experts, along with 2) explicit questioning of the objectivity of the series as well as 3) concluding that the allegation that Burked killed his sister is "total BS." A *CNN* commentator is quoted calling the *CBS* show shameful, reckless and worthy of a "Fake News Award."

Counterintuitively, perhaps, episode two of the series remains available, including the cliff-hanger in the final four minutes of the almost two-hour episode. At the denouement during episode two, the experts gathered around the table are apparently unanimous on camera that it *appears* **JonBenét's family didn't want law enforcement to resolve this case.**[9]

Layer #3

It's really through this lens that we need to read everything the Ramseys say and do.

CABELL: *When you return to Boulder, you will sit down with the Boulder police?*

JOHN [Nods, then shakes his head]: *Oh, absolutely. Absolutely. We want them to know every-thing possible...[trails off].*

PATSY: *Everything.*

JOHN: *That could help them.*

PATSY: *Whatever they want [head bouncing], whatever anyone wants, we will co-operate.*

It's really through this lens of secretly not wanting law enforcement to get anywhere, that we should look at how the polygraph tests came about, and why they took three years to achieve, and the results themselves were both dubious and inconclusive.

It's through this prism of secretly hoping to frustrate an investigation, that we need to look at documentaries with names like:

Hunting JonBenét's Killer

Because it's really the opposite. It's about not hunting. It's about not finding her killer. It's about not really investigating anything that matters.

When we bear in mind Layer #1 and #2, it feels not only logical but inevitable that something as vital as the last photo would be withheld from the media, the public and who knows, perhaps law enforcement too, for 23 years. Because the idea isn't to solve this case, it's to control how the stories about the case are told, who tells it, when and where. The Ramseys, or perhaps just one of them, wants to be in any story told about the Ramseys, and if not, an effort seems to be made to discredit the story, either through litigation or by pretending that it doesn't exist, and is therefore of no significance.

How the last photo fits into the fabric of the case, and the pageantry surrounding this case is almost as interesting as the last photo itself. We begin our analysis of the last photo by acknowledging, first of all, what the last photo is not. It's not <u>the previous last photo</u>. It's not JonBenét looking relaxed and happy and loved. She's not smiling, and she's not necessarily not smiling. The image is slightly unfocused, and JonBenét appears between expressions. Oddly, JonBenét is almost unrecognizable in this final photo. In those big, wide eyes are so many untold stories, and unfortunately, many stories that will ultimately never be told.

The image is tightly cropped in such a way that we can't see anyone else in the room, and it's hard to make our what she's wearing, where she's standing [or if she's lying on a wooden floor] or what exactly she's doing. In other words, this isn't a carrot, it's a piece of a carrot. Ironically, none of that really matters.

What matters is the bow in her hair. The same bow is in her hair when she's photographed on the carpet in the Ramsey house, dead.

Garrotted.

Bludgeoned over the head.

What does it prove? It proves two things.

1. JonBenét never went to bed that night.

2. If six-year-old JonBenét never went to bed, and she ended up dead because of the actions of someone in the house, then *those in whose custody and care and guardianship* JonBenét found herself were indirectly responsible for what happened to her. Put another way, if the bow had been removed and JonBenét put to bed as most six-year-olds should have been, and would have been late on Christmas Night, she likely would still be alive today. That she wasn't is why she isn't, and this is the shameful aspect that's been hiding under the dark silhouette beneath Blunder's bright, blinking Christmas Star all these years.

Bedwetting and Pageant Trophies

"He is happiest, be he king or peasant, who finds peace in his home." — Johann Wolfgang von Goethe

If the Ramseys neglected JonBenét on the night of her murder, and at no other time, or on very few other occasions, it's hard to imagine a jury would fault them for anything. Accidents happen. Bad things happen to good people. But there is a difference between accidents and bad things, and *really* bad things. What happened to JonBenét – her death – wasn't just an accident, and it wasn't random. She was tortured and beaten to death. Her skull was brutally split open and her throat cruelly garrotted by someone exerting incredible force.

Whoever killed the little girl clearly wanted to do what they did. It can't be an accidental bludgeoning given the extreme force of the blow. It can't be an accidental garrotting given the cruel depth of the garrotte into the little girl's tender throat. One thing that we can speculate on that plays into the "defense" of the perpetrator – it's possible that the idea wasn't so much to murder JonBenét but to *silence* her at a critical moment. We will deal with the import of this particular statement in the final chapter.

For now let's ask a few simple and straightforward questions, and then attempt to find the most qualified insiders to answer them.

A. NEGLECT

1. Was JonBenét a neglected child?

2. Was Burke a neglected child?

B. BEDWETTING

3. Was the one child more or less neglected than the other?

4. If the one child was more or less neglected, how might this play out in the *schema* of this case?

It may be putting the cart before the horse, but the Grand Jury, certainly, felt enough evidence had been led to indict on the grounds of child neglect. Were the Grand Jury justified? On December 16th, 2016, a grand juror who saw the original evidence first-hand spoke to *ABC* news.

*"I saw that there was a little girl dressed up with, in my opinion, a sexual persona, and it disgusted me. [But] there is no way that I would have been able to say, 'Beyond a reasonable doubt, this is the person.".... The juror said he believes that there was enough evidence to indict John and Patsy Ramsey for a crime, but he doesn't think they would have been convicted. Still, he says **the grand jury did recommend charges against John and Patsy Ramsey, indicating the jurors believed they placed JonBenét in a situation resulting in her death.***

Whatever we make of this anonymous juror's opinion, it's clear JonBenét did have a *sexual persona* which was out of the norm for most if not all children of her age. One could even go so far to say the creating – the staging [on stage] – of this persona was a kind of neglectful abuse in its own right. But that's not what we're driving at. We're driving at the ordinary definition. And if there was ordinary neglect of one or both kids, was it a little neglect or was it chronic?

We get credible reinforcement for the abuse JonBenét suffered from an unexpected quarter – Lin Wood. On the <u>PBWorks site devoted to JonBenét Ramsey</u>, in the section dealing with "Evidence of Sexual Assault" the <u>Ramsey vs CBS defamation case</u> gets top billing, and with it, Lin Wood's argument:

"The evidence clearly demonstrated that JonBenét's murderer also sexually assaulted her: (1) <u>there was blood on JonBenét's underwear</u> and the entrance of her vagina; (2) JonBenét's hymen had been freshly broken, likely close in time to her death; (3) forensic pathologists that examined her found that she had been penetrated; and (4) fragments of wood that matched the garrotte handle were found in her vagina."

Going by this version, it sounds like JonBenét was raped, with blood dripping everywhere. There were tiny amounts of blood recovered from the white blanket, from the panties and from JonBenét's clothing. The truth lies somewhere between Wood's version, which he's laid on quite thick, and no abuse whatsoever.

The autopsy[10] provides a different portrait compared to Wood's. Where Wood refers to a broken hymen, <u>the autopsy refers to an "eroded surface."</u> Where Wood refers to finding that JonBenét had been penetrated, the autopsy referred to vascular congestion and chronic inflammation. As a result, going by the autopsy evidence alone, some experts have dismissed the notion of sexual abuse altogether, citing the inflammation and the abrasion to the hymen as just ordinary wear-and-tear associated with run-of-the-mill vaginitis.

It's easy to get confused by all the toing and froing from the various pundits. The bottom-line, and one I've stressed over the span of more than three trilogies, is that one can't compare sexual assault or the genital situation of adults to small children. By the same token, a six-year-old uniquely oversexualized child with *any* kind of vaginal aberration is certainly cause for concern. The fact that the autopsy mentions it means there is more than passing significance to it – not in the pedophile predator sense of the Ramseys, Wood and Detective Lou Smit,[11] but also not in the harmless vaginitis sense of the various experts that have prognosticated over this case. It's somewhere in-between. And in that somewhere inbetweenness we see how if there was abuse, and if it was protracted [and the vaginal injuries appear to show that it was protracted] then so was the neglect. And in a scenario of protracted neglect one can imagine a creeping chronic recklessness that can, on certain occasions like Christmas where one might be even less on point than usual, that neglect may pave the way for something not only tragic, but inevitable.

It's understandable that the Ramseys *et al* would emphasize a sexual deviant in this case, as this would by default exonerate Burke, at a minimum. If JonBenét's vaginal trauma is sketched as seemingly similar to that perpetrated by an adult, thus an adult sexual assault on a child, then clearly a child cannot be implicated. The thing is it's not. It's not an adult sexual assault. JonBenét's hymen was partially intact. The 6mm perforation in the child's hymen could be explained by another child's finger, or less likely, her own.

It's easier to make the argument that JonBenét was neglected in terms of her general health, or lack of, than specifically making the case that sexual abuse was either permitted or not known when it ought to have been. In the latter case, the trilogies prior to this narrative have exhaustively investigated the sleeping habits of the children, amid a holocaust of bedwetting and scatological behavior, particularly from Burke.

One of the housekeepers spoke of Burke smearing his shit on the walls, on JonBenét's Christmas gifts, and in one instance leaving a grapefruit sized ball of dung.

According to the *Daily Mail*:

Ex-housekeeper Linda Hoffman-Pugh also remembered a time when she uncovered "faecal material the size of a grapefruit on the sheets" in the bed of JonBenét. After they sealed off JonBenét's room, the crime scene technicians went through it, they apparently found feces smeared on a box of candy she had got for Christmas." Forensic pathologist Dr Werner Spitz revealed Burke had spread feces on a bathroom wall in the family home.

It shouldn't be necessary to emphasize that no child would smear their own Christmas gifts with their own excrement. But a severely jealous, <u>mischievous</u>,[12] capricious, and <u>perhaps neglected child</u>, might do that to a sibling on Christmas, especially a sibling who is usurping his role as the Golden Child, and stealing the lion's share of attention that was all his, once upon a time.

When we go back to once upon a time, when it was Burke's time, his former nanny Shirley Brady sketches a totally different portrait. On January 10th, 1997 Brady told the *Daily Camera*:

*I was the housekeeper and nanny [when the Ramseys lived in Atlanta in the late 80's] to their little son who was born while I was there. **Both are devoted parents and I was crazy about Burke.** I used to rock him to sleep; he loved Handel's Messiah's Halleluiah Chorus. He loved for me to read to him. I have in my heart and mind **so many happy memories of the whole family** including grandparents and aunts. When I saw that little coffin and the grieving parents, I was stunned. Who could do such a violent, crazy deed? It is plain insanity for anyone to even think a family member would have done it. **After Mr. Ramsey's oldest daughter died, JonBenét was his salvation to go on from his sorrow, losing his oldest.***

On October 15th, 1999 Brady provided another update to the back-story in an exclusive with the *Denver Post*:

Brady came to work for JonBenét's parents…when they were living in Atlanta…before they moved to Boulder in 1991.[13] *She initially was hired when…Burke, was born, and then she helped raise JonBenét until she was 6 months old. "In the three years I was in that house, there was never an argument, never voices raised," Brady said.*

If Brady knew the Ramseys as a happy family, a few things happened after those heady early days of family bliss. First of all there was the move from Atlanta to Boulder in **1991**, when Burke was four. That alone would have been traumatic. Dad focused on his expanding business, mom focussed on decorating their new home, and Burke having to do without his beloved nanny, Miss Brady. Just as the little boy was settling in in Colorado, there was Beth's death on January 8th, **1992**, when Burke was almost five.

This untimely event made John unconsciously gravitate to his youngest child and only surviving daughter, and away from his second son. At the time of Beth's accident, JonBenét – born in August 1990 – was just over two years old. Burke Ramsey, whose birthday is January 27th, 1987, as mentioned above was almost five at the time.

The following year – **1993**[14] – things got even worse, when Patsy was diagnosed with stage 4 ovarian cancer. Patsy's condition and frequent absences from home for treatment likely diluted the attention that had flowed to Burke to a mere trickle.

In **1994** there was some respite, Patsy fought back against her cancer, came home but instead of *being back home* with Burke, after an exploratory visit to a Little Miss America contest with her mother Nedra, Patsy started entering JonBenét in pageants.[15] That meant focussing all her attention on her daughter, and travelling frequently with her.

In the **summer of 1994**, JonBenét was struck on the upper left cheek or just below the eye socket by Burke swinging a golf club. Since Patsy took JonBenét to a plastic surgeon once the injury and bruising had healed in October, it's possible this injury was inflicted a few weeks earlier, in August 1994. It's also possible the injury wasn't accidental, and happened on or close to JonBenét birthday [August 6th].

JonBenét won her first competition that same year, when she was three going on four [and Burke seven] at the Colorado State All-Star Kids Pageant in April 1994. A few months later, in July, JonBenét won Little Miss Charlevoix.

Then, in **October 1995** JonBenét won Miss Colorado Sunburst. But for almost a year following the eye injury incident, JonBenét Ramsey pageant resume remained on idle.

In **1996**, between ages five and six JonBenét came second in the Sunburst National Pageant [held in August] and won the Colorado Little Miss Christmas pageant on December 17th. Five days later, on December 22nd, JonBenét entered another pageant, and won a medal for talent at the Colorado All-stars Christmas Pageant.[16]

In the last two years of her life, JonBenét quickly became a fully-fledged pageant princess with a bunch of prestigious titles and trophies to her name including Little Miss Colorado, America's Royale Miss [July 1996] and National Tiny Miss Beauty. And where was Burke? Burke was at home whittling, and playing with his poop.

Where Burke was once the apple of his family's eye [before JonBenét came along], it was hard not to see JonBenét as his rival. As soon as she arrived, his life turned sucky. Given the trials and traumas, and the gyres and gyrations within the family, we can see how the neglect of the children could be at times inevitable, and at other times, under circumstances of their own making, they may have simply been distracted by the slings and arrows of outrageous fortune. John Ramsey gross-ing over $1 billion in turnover through his Access Graphics business, and Patsy's successful campaigns on the pageant circuit weren't neces-sarily situations outside of the Ramseys control, but one can imagine Burke feeling like he was the only one not really going anywhere. And it wasn't like Burke could put on a coat of lipstick, wave his arms on stage and become _fabulous_.

Even if JonBenét was getting the lion's share of attention, it didn't mean it was good attention, or good for her. It also didn't mean that she wasn't being neglected as a child, even if she was the toast of child pageantry. Ironically, despite the perfectly coiffed hair, the sparkling lipstick, the crisp polka dot outfits, wide-brimmed hats and all the rest, the daily ritual started with the stench of urine. In three years JonBenét visited her paediatrician, Dr. Beuf, 30 times. On Decem-ber 17th, between 17:00 and 18:00 Patsy called Dr. Beuf's office three times. Possibly JonBenét had vaginitis again, right before another pageant. Not only was JonBenét's health in a poor state, her hygiene was abysmal.[17]

It's possible the vaginitis led to a musical beds situation in the home, and that led to bed sharing and possibly molestation. By allowing the vaginitis – and also the bedwetting – to go on for as long as it did, this placed JonBenét in an awkward situation. Once she wet her bed she simply went to sleep in another bed. But _Burke was also wetting his bed_. Eventually a situation would – and did – arise where both children got into the same bed.

So it seems either the parents were aware of this and did nothing, or were unaware of it and did nothing. But it's in this area where the neglect not only of one child but both children opens the door to one child who'd already been abusing the other, taking matters further, without fear of parental interference, or intervention.

And suddenly it becomes all too clear why that bow was still in JonBenét's hair way past the bedtime of a six-year-old. JonBenét never went to bed that night because *she was never put to bed*, not on December 25th, or on any other night, and neither was Burke. Do you follow? They put *themselves* to bed just like they always did, except on Christmas Night there was reason to stay up late and play while everyone else was somewhere else, perhaps asleep, perhaps still celebrating their outrageous fortune.

The Flood of 95 and a Flash of Anger

Steve Thomas: *Patsy, when were you last in that cellar basement room prior to Christmas?*

Patsy: *Prior to Christmas?*

Thomas: *Yes, ma'am.*

Patsy: *Well, I was there, I was down there a lot on the 24th wrapping, and I was there on the 25th wrapping...* — Boulder Police Interview, April 30th, 1997

Since the Ramseys aren't telling, our best peek into what was really going on inside the Ramsey home comes from the housekeepers. Like Linda Wilcox

Wilcox was interviewed by Boulder police officer Jane Harmer because she had a key to the Ramsey home, and had had it for two years. She was also palm printed, but no other evidence was taken – no handwriting, no hair. Wilcox said if she'd been asked she would have freely given the police samples.

Now, when we run through an anecdote from Wilcox from <u>Peter Boyles' radio show on July 21st, 1998</u> [it's quite long], we're not focused on trying to find anything dark or sinister. We simply want to peek inside the Boulder home, and get a sense of what it felt like in 1995.

From there we'll go on to deal with the flash of anger. In that second section we're more interested in something that might be twisted and untrue. Worth playing for?

1. The Flood of '95

WILCOX: *Yes, the flood. That was an interesting one. What had happened, Jay…was [in] John's bathroom. They each had their own bathroom, John and Patsy. And, neither used the other. It was too weird.*

Let's pause for a moment on this. The personalities and habits are important conduits into the psychologies of their brood. Like father like son. Like mother like daughter, right? What does this bathroom *apartheid* tell us about the Ramseys? It suggests that they were used to having their own spaces, and having their spaces to themselves and having their space customised just the way they wanted. In a word this was a family of four, and each individual member was pretty spoiled.

What does it mean to be *spoiled*: it's when someone is so damaged by getting everything they want, when things don't go there way, they *still* try to get their way, including by lying, cheating or who knows what.

And, as we're about to see, they weren't just spoiled but *spoiled rotten*; they were used to someone else cleaning up if a mess was made, and a giant waterworks on the scale of Paddington Bear was in the making here.

WILCOX: *The housepainter had been painting. It was over Thanksgiving break. It had been warm. He'd been painting and he left the window open. We got one of those big wind storms. The wind blew the shutter open just enough to hit the [long slim] handle on the hot water faucet [of the shower] and so water started running through that shower head. But it didn't reach the bathtub. It went off the side, and onto the floor. It ran for like three days, hot water.*

Something like this, then. Wilcox goes on to describe the deluge building up and flowing into Patsy's lounge. Then it penetrated the ceiling and poured into John Andrew's room downstairs.

WILCOX: *It had gone...all the way to the first floor guest bathroom. It did approximately $20,000 worth of damage.*

Notice Wilcox's choice of words here. Not so much that the water flooded John Andrew's *en suite* bathroom [which it did], but that it went all the way into the guest bathroom behind it on the first floor. The first floor isn't a mistaken reference to the ground floor. The guest bathroom Wilcox is referring to here is JonBenét's bathroom of course. So why does Wilcox refer to it as the guest bathroom? Probably because when the Flood of '95 happened, JonBenét wasn't using the guest bedroom. We know from Patsy that JonBenét started off using Melinda's bedroom [next door to Burke's], and immediately opposite the stairs leading up to the master bedroom of the parents on the third floor.

And yet for reasons unknown between the summer of 1995 and the winter of 1996 JonBenét had moved to the far side of the house; not only about as far from Burke's room as she could possibly get, but also – perhaps significantly – far from the master bedroom above Burke's room. FBI Profiler John Douglas refers to the distance of JonBenét's room to the Ramsey's bedroom in an interview specifically to exonerate them.

MSNBC REPORTER: *[Douglas] knew that whoever committed the crime had to have intimate knowledge of the Ramseys' million dollar home.*

DOUGLAS: *What struck me as unusual [camera pans over Burke's bedroom] is that the bedrooms...the mother and father's bedrooms...was so far away on that third floor [gestures], that – even if you weren't a sound sleeper – you'd have difficulty hearing any noise on the second floor. Because it is so far removed.*

I'm not sure I agree completely with Douglas on this point. JonBenét's bedroom is far from the master bedroom, true, but Burke's bedroom isn't. Also, the bedroom moves continuously along the third floor so that it's effectively above JonBenét's bedroom as well. The third floor bathroom, dressing room and study are all directly above JonBenét's room, and a likely space where the parents spent time when they weren't sleeping. It's also the most likely space they would have been late on Christmas Night after a dinner party with friends. One could also make the argument that if the Ramseys were awake and not in bed, but were on the third floor, then it would be Burke's room that would be furthest from the living area, including "Patsy's lounge." And so for this *someone* who had intimate knowledge not only of the house but the habits of the parents to get up to mischief without being heard, Burke's room could certainly qualify as a better alternative in a scenario where the Ramseys were upstairs and still awake and the idea was to not be easily seen or heard.

It may also be that JonBenét didn't wish to sleep on Christmas Night, or couldn't sleep, and so she ventured from the one side of the second floor to the next – to Burke's side – to participate in the post-Christmas gameplay. As children do.

Now let's go back to the housekeeper.

WILCOX: *[The Ramseys] were due back in town but because of fog in Atlanta, they couldn't fly back that day. I went to call [John Ramsey's] office and I looked through the top drawer of his desk to see if I could find a business card for Access Graphics. And **I'm upstairs in his office,** since there's a phone in there, looking for it. [But] I couldn't get an outside line. I'd been there almost two years at this time and I didn't' know you had to dial 1 to get an outside line…So I got in my car and I found a pay phone and called his secretary…I think her name was Laurie.*[18]

Wilcox's inability to get an outside line also demystifies the possibility that some stranger at the Christmas party, or child, on December 23rd dialled 911 by mistake. Probably the call was made by one of the Ramseys or, less likely, a very close friend. Effectively whoever made that call on December 23rd would have had to dial 1-911 to get through. The numbers one 1 and 9 are typically on the opposite side of most numerical keypads, including and especially telephones.

WILCOX: *I got a hold of [Laurie]...I explained to her that I was having trouble with the phone...she told me to look around...I couldn't close the [bathroom] window. It was really jammed because the water had made it swell. I couldn't close the window and this was [at] eight in the morning. Well, I spent the whole day there. Especially [in] John Andrew's room. It was the worst [affected], it was flooded. I was using the steam cleaner to extract the water. [Then] at about 8 o'clock that night...[the Ramseys] got home...I remember we walked up to the master bedroom and I showed them [John's] bathroom and what had happened. And I said, 'Oh I can't close the window.' Well John gets in the bathtub, he yanked open the shutter and he slammed the window down. He's standing there in the bathtub with his stocking feet. I'd gotten [rid of] most of the water, but it would like creep up between the tiles, and he got his feet wet. He got really ticked. You could see it in his face. It was like his eyes changed color he was so mad. But he has extreme self-control...[And then] he just very calmly said, 'Man I'm gonna fire Jay right now, he's gonna pay for this.'*

John's temperament is important here. He arrives home late and night to discover his million dollar home has been seriously inundated with water. His own bedroom and the floor below have been so extensively damaged remodelling would be required. And yet Boulder's soon-to-be Entrepreneur of the Year[19] remains cool and calm, cooler and calmer than most people would having suffered $20 000 in damages.

2. The Flash of Anger

The flash of anger isn't a reference to John. John Ramsey strikes one as the strong, silent type, doesn't he? If he's an introvert, then Patsy was the extravert. Then what about Burke and JonBenét?

Clearly JonBenét was an extravert like her mom. And Burke? Was he more like his dad or like his mom? Introverted? Extraverted? Or a bit of both? Curiously, the golf club incident in Burke's backstory was completely missed during both John and Patsy's interviews with the Boulder police on April 30th, 1997.[20]

KANE:...*Did you talk to someone about getting your golf clubs [from the house]?*

JOHN: *No. Absolutely not.*

KANE: *Okay [not pursuing the question]. From what I have read, JonBenét had an injury at one time to her face. What do you know about that?*

JOHN: *Burke was up...*

Whoah! Just play back that again.

KANE: *JonBenét had an injury at one time to her face. What do you know about that?*

JOHN: *Burke was up...*

John's absolutely clear in putting injury to JonBenét's face and Burke together, isn't he? It's not just that though, it's the reference to golf clubs. So it's really the injury to JonBenét's face, Burke and golf clubs. Still, John doesn't ask for clarification. Instead, he gets straight to the point with Kane.

JOHN: *Burke was up at the lake...and Burke was in the yard swinging a golf club, and she walked up either in front of him or behind him, I was not there, and she got clobbered. It was a pure accident.*

Sure. Accidents happen all the time, right?

KANE: *Where did you hear about that?*

JOHN: *Oh, Patsy called me.*

KANE: *You were out of town?*

John said he couldn't remember where he was. His wife and two children were somewhere, and he was somewhere else, sort of a repeat of what happened on Christmas Night and the day after Christmas.

Kane lets the incident slide. He probably has to, if he wants the Ramseys to keep talking. Touch briefly on a few questions, gloss over a few answers, then move on. So Kane moves on to another potential incident. Another injury.

KANE: *I guess this was another – Burke went to school after this. Had a black eye. Do you know anything about that?*

Kane seems to be testing, or checking, whether John may have physically harmed either of his children. Did John hit JonBenét in the face? No chance, he wasn't in town. Okay then what about Burke's black eye? No chance of that either, it was a baseball that Patsy threw at Burke. Bear in mind the jury ultimately voted to charge the Ramseys with child abuse, so these questions are extremely relevant.

JOHN: *Um, he got – <u>there's a picture of him in his baseball uniform with a real shiner</u> and he had gotten a black eye playing baseball.*

John's reference to a particular picture of Burke wearing his baseball clothes is very clear, and very specific. John's also not in the dark about what Kane's referring to here. But it's not entirely accurate that Burke's wearing a "baseball uniform." In fact he's wearing a long-sleeved collared shirt and what appears to be jeans. He's got his cap on the wrong way, and he's wearing a baseball glove. Arguably the only uniform he's wearing is the glove. This image was taken in the spring of 1996. That makes it very relevant to the events at hand. JonBenét, standing behind Burke, also wearing a cap facing the wrong way [emulating her big brother], appears to be sitting on a bicycle and wearing bicycle gloves. The image is cropped in such a way that the handlebars of the bicycle – this bicycle[21] – are almost impossible to see.

Without looking at the image, and it's not clear whether Kane had, or whether he'd simply been told about the incident, it's easy to give John the benefit of the doubt here. And his story adds up. It makes sense.

JOHN: *He [Burke] was a fielder and [roleplaying] "I got it, I got, I got it," CLUNK.*

KANE: *Was it during a game?*

JOHN: *Yeah.*

It sounds like Burke was playing a baseball game, perhaps at school, when, during the course of the game, a high ball struck him on the noggin, right?

KANE: *As part of –*

JOHN [Interrupting]: *Yes, it was part of the league he was in, a practice or a game.*

Oh so now Burke was in a uniform, but not necessary playing a match, he might have been practicing.

KANE: *You weren't there?*

JOHN: *No.*

But this time Kane doesn't let the question slide quite as easily as the clobbering with the golf stick JonBenét received.

KANE: *Where did you hear about it?*

JOHN: *Patsy told me about it.*

KANE: *Okay.*

JOHN [Adding]: *But he got conked by a....because ball. It should have been in the glove but he missed it.*

KANE: *You never heard it was Patsy that threw the ball?*

JOHN: *No.*

KANE: *Okay.*

JOHN: *It wasn't. Never heard that. It wasn't her; it was a fly ball.*

So what's interesting here is Kane seems to be suggesting that maybe Patsy threw the baseball purposefully at Burke and it hit him in the eye. Again, even if John's statement is true, given what the Grand Jury ultimately voted to indict the parents with, the line of questioning is certainly interesting. It's a case of:

Did Patsy do something?

Now let's deal with Patsy, and the golf incident. Bear in mind this question didn't come up with Patsy either during the first go-around on the last day of April 1997, during the first interview with Boulder Police Department.

HANEY: *Okay. There was mention…of a situation where [Burke] apparently hit JonBenét with a golf club up <u>at Charlevoix</u>?*

PATSY: *Yes.*

Yes. *Just yes.*

HANEY [Pressing]: *Could you tell us about that?*

PATSY: *He was taking a practice swing, he was just a little guy, he was two or three, or two and a half, and he was – it was our first summer there, how young they were there.*

Patsy says very little about the incident before she starts minimizing it. It couldn't have been a severe injury, or a hard blow, if it was a practice swing. [John also emphasized it was a practice swing]. How did they know it was a practice swing? Were they there? Did they see it? Then Patsy makes it into a toddler thing. Burke was a toddler of two, or three, waddling about clumsily – you get the picture. But if Burke was two, that would make it 1989 and JonBenét wouldn't have been born yet. If Burke was three, that would make it 1990, JonBenét's would have been a new-born in August, but the house in Charlevoix hadn't even been bought yet.[22] It was bought at the end of the year in 1992, when JonBenét's was two-years-old and Burke was almost six-year-old.

Patsy claims the incident happened on *their first summer there* but without specifying a date. But then the investigator presses her on precisely when.

HANEY: *About what year would that have been?*

PATSY RAMSEY: *That was '93, I believe.*

In the summer of '93 Burke was six-and-a-half-years-old, not two or three, and JonBenét was two going on three. But according to reports in *Vanity Fair*:

[Burke] had hit JonBenét with a golf club about **a year and a half before the murder.**

That would be mid-1994, shortly after JonBenét entered her first pageants, and close to her 4th birthday. Judith Phillips, a former family friend and photographer of the Ramsey family confirms this date. In an episode of *The Case Of: JonBenét Ramsey* Phillips remarks about Burke's temper.

"I think [he] had a bad temper. It's like he had a chip on his shoulder. He had hit JonBenét...It was probably a year and a half [before the murder]. They were playing in the yard and apparently he hit her with the golf club, right here [Phillips indicates an area under the eye]. She [Patsy]

says the kids were playing, Burke lost his temper and hit her with a golf club."

If the Ramseys knew this and did nothing, or if they knew this and it happened again, and again, and JonBenét eventually lost her life because it happened again, when both JonBenét and Burke were meant to be under their custody, their supervision, and their protection, then certainly, the Ramseys would have a case to answer for. But it all hangs on the word "if".

Of course if there's a mosaic of neglect in other areas, then the if starts to fall away, doesn't it?

Dead Dogs and Dirty Panties

"My initial reaction was, a stranger didn't kill that child." — Linda Wilcox, <u>Ramsey housekeeper to Peter Boyles</u>, July 1998

I t's the nature of the Christmas Star to monopolize all the attention, isn't it? The star floating in the air attracts our attention, or interest, our hope. And why not. It's bright, it's golden-white, and in the cold and dark of winter we want to be warmed by comforting sights.

But in this story we ought not to be distracted by comforting lights. We must peer beyond the dazzling Christmas Star to what lies underneath it, to what shadowy apparition hidden in the dark, holds it aloft. It's the brightness of the star that prevents us from seeing the furtive silhouette under it, but once we've cottoned on to this idea of tuning out the bright star, the jagged inky thing below it slowly comes into view.

The dark forest that we're trying to make out, tucked inside the sleepy shadows of night, is this idea of chronic neglect. Instead of trying to look too hard into areas that are hidden or concealed from view, let's venture along another branch, and see what's fairly plain, hiding in the half-light.

In Linda Hoffman-Pugh's aborted book about the Ramseys, <u>published as a single blog post</u>, the housekeeper who was employed at the time of the murder provides the most prescient and penetrating insight of all. As one would expect. In fact Hoffman-Pugh was meant to come in later that day, once the Ramseys had left on another fancy all-frills adventure, to clean up the Christmas mess on the day after Christmas. Linda had to clean up the discarded gingerbread houses, make the unmade beds, and gather up the piles of Christmas paper trash. But instead of coming in that day, she was told not to. Because on December 26th a little girl had been turned into trash, and stowed in a basement for someone else to find, or not find, to clean-up, or be disposed of.

According to the housekeeper, in the fourteen months she was employed by the Ramseys she never once witnessed the "slightest affection" – between John and Patsy. The housekeeper claimed she:

"...never once saw [the Ramseys] embrace. I never once saw them hold hands, I never once saw them a kiss, or hug, or use words or terms of endearment, or speak to one another with any warmth or tenderness. Not once. Not ever! In fact, I don't think I've ever been around a married couple who looked so uncomfortable together. Or a couple who were as cold to one another, as these two."

One might say that's merely the opinion of a disgruntled house-keeper. Or one might say if the couple were so lacking in tenderness to one another, what could it have been like being their children? If the housekeeper believed they neglected one another in such obvious ways, why would it be outlandish to imagine their children might feel neglected in some way as well?

When Peter Boyles asked the other housekeeper to expand on the relationship the Ramseys had with her, it conformed – sort of – to the impression sketched by Hoffman-Pugh.

From ACandyRose.com:

BOYLES:…*it's my understanding that the Ramseys would speak in front of anyone about anything because* **the help was seen as part of the furniture***… is that fair?…What do you think their relationship was like?*

In her response, Wilcox referred to Boyle's description of the "help" [in other words, how the Ramseys saw her and others like her as furniture] as "a relatively fair assessment." Then she expanded on the issue more explicitly.

WILCOX: *As far as I was concerned,* **I was furniture.**

What the housekeeper's saying effectively is:

The way I experienced the Ramseys – they treated me like furniture. I didn't matter. I wasn't important.

But what about Hoffman-Pugh's assessment of how they treated each other? If John was cool and calm, was he like that with everyone?

WILCOX: *[Their] relationship was amiable and polite for the most part.* **It was a business relationship.** *They didn't [what?]…they weren't affectionate.*

If they weren't affectionate to one another, and treated their housekeepers like furniture, how did they treat their children?

WILCOX: *They didn't act like a married couple…they [seemed like] business associates. That's pretty much how it was. She was like his secretary, not his wife. As far as I can tell from making the bed, the sheets weren't…*

We won't deal with the bedwetting although it's clear more than one housekeeper seemed burdened with this almost on a daily basis.[23] Instead, let's turn to a proxy for the children, the pet dog Jacques. How was Jacques treated by the family? In short – not well. The dog is *sort of* like a parable for JonBenét.

From ACandyRose.com:

WILCOX: *Patsy didn't want a dog. And, she didn't want JonBenét to have a dog. This particular **dog didn't get the potty training thing down very well, he tended to leave puddles.** He was pretty much **relegated to the wood floor at the bottom of the spiral staircase.** His name was Jacques, a little guy, cute little fur ball. Well, one day the dog went to the vet and [never] came back. The dog that [came back from] the vet was smaller than the dog that left.*

Everything that Wilcox says here whispers neglect.

Patsy didn't want a dog.

But they had a dog. So what happened to the unwanted dog? In short, it got sick and was either given away, or put down.

And, she didn't want JonBenét to have a dog.

Why wouldn't Patsy want JonBenét to have a dog? Possibly because dogs were dirty, and would make her little girl dirty and full of dog hair. Possibly because dogs were just too much damn work, and who was going to look after it? Not Patsy. Not John. Not JonBenét. Not Burke. Ultimately no one. Isn't that chronic neglect?

*This particular **dog didn't get the potty training thing down very well, he tended to leave puddles.***

So even the dog was wetting its bed, and leaving excrement all over the house. It's difficult to be more explicit about neglect – of any living creature – than to allow of scenario of excrement and urine building up in one's own home.

*He was pretty much **relegated to the wood floor at the bottom of the spiral staircase.***

He was neglected. He wasn't a happy dog, he wasn't trained and he wasn't allowed to hang out with the family much.

His name was Jacques, a little guy, cute little fur ball. Well, one day the dog went to the vet and [never] came back.

After a long period of neglect, Jacques's fate ended unhappily ever after, just as JonBenét's did.

When Wilcox confronted Patsy about the New Jacques, Patsy conspiratorially told the furniture, smirking perhaps, "Sssh. Don't tell anyone. No one else knows."

In terms of John's relationship with the dog, Wilcox is pretty clear as well.

WILCOX: *John took no responsibility for [the dog] whatsoever. He tolerated it at best. And, if it got anything of his, heaven forbid. I don't know this, but I think they got rid of the dog because when they were in Michigan, they were busy with pageants. They were doing other things and* **there was no one to look after the dog.** *I think they gave it to the neighbors when they left for the summer because they didn't want to hassle with the dog.*

It turns out <u>the New Jacques was given away</u> just like the Old Jacques became ill and was given away. There is no way to be plainer on the treatment of the dog than Wilcox's words, when she says:

They were doing other things and there was no one to look after the dog.

Why wouldn't the same thing apply – generally – to the children?

There was no one to look after ~~the dog~~ *the kids.*

According to Wilcox, this is true. Wilcox claims JonBenét "got no affection at all" when she was little [perhaps while her mother had cancer] except from the nanny.[24]

WILCOX: *Until [JonBenét] started to perform or produce,* **she was basically ignored.** *At one point, John was complaining because he had to* *get her dressed one morning because Suzanne had been out of town. He couldn't find any clothes [for JonBenét] that matched. The reason was,* **she was wearing cast-offs from Burke because she didn't have any clothes of her own.**

JonBenét had fancy outfits for the stage, and for Christmas parties. <u>But she didn't have proper clothes</u> – and so much besides - that any ordinary little girl should have.

Pageantry Around the Ransom Note

"The Miss America Pageant reinforces a belief that women are merely how they look and how they please." — Gloria Steinem

On December 21ˢᵗ, 2016, after reaching out unsuccessfully to HLN, I wrote a rant and posted it on *Shakedown*. It went like this:

Sometimes the most obvious truth is the most recondite. The biggest smoke from the biggest gun occurred right at the beginning of this case. The first police officer on the scene arrived at the Ramsey home before 06:00, before dawn. He noticed <u>trace snow had covered the exterior of the home, and surrounded all of it</u>. Nowhere was there any evidence of footprints leading away from the house. The officer knew before entering the house that the crime had been reported as a kidnapping. You're approaching a home at more than an hour and twenty minutes before the crack of dawn with the idea of someone stealing a child out of the home. The first thing you're going to notice is why that doesn't make any sense. **There are no footprints on the virgin snow leading to the front door, and no footprints anywhere else.**

The fact that the Ramsey case went from one surrounded by untrammelled snow to a genuine mystery is perhaps the biggest mystery of all. Of course it's *not* a mystery, it never was, what it is is pure pageantry and some of the most expensive public relations money can buy. That's what made the Ramsey case appear to be mysterious at all. And the prime instrument of that pageantry is the Ransom Note. It's not real, everybody knows it, and yet – like Christmas – it's part of the *mythos*. <u>A once ridiculous unreality</u> has evolved into something familiar, and ultimately, charming. Just like Christmas, we can no longer see the Ransom Note for what it really is. Like Christmas, when we look at the Ransom Note we no longer see the Ransom Note, we just feel the *mythos* around it.

But True Crime Rocket Science can see-through the mythos. The three-page Ransom Note – the mother of all ransom notes – distinguishes the Ramsey case from all others. Like all pageantry, the Ramsey Ransom Note is simultaneously compelling and a farce. Over the course of 23 years of true crime followers obsessing over this case, most have been duped by the Ransom Note even when they've correctly identified it as fakery. The fakery is obvious, just as the Christmas *mythos* is obvious. What's less obvious, but not necessarily rocket science either, is the why behind the fakery. The psychology of the thing. The psychology of the pageantry. Why is it there? What function does it serve?

So it's not a question of seeing the various trees that's the smoking gun here, it's seeing the Ransom Note as a *woods* in and of itself.

Let me explain.

The Ransom Note is not only the best evidence of what *didn't happen* to JonBenét we have, it's also the best artefact telling us exactly <u>who and what we're dealing with</u>. Without deciphering the Ransom Note in detail, or even at all, it suffices to say the note in sum is at turns credible but also ridiculous. Just like the Ramseys.

The Ramsey case is like that too. Credible and ridiculous. The house, <u>elegant and stately on the outside</u>, is <u>ridiculous on the</u>

inside. The <u>historic, soaring triangular gables on the outside are graceful</u>, the squat block of renovated mishmash <u>hoiked</u> into the side of the structure is not. <u>The kitchen is a smorgasbord of clutter</u>, the basement is a labyrinth so extensive and <u>chaotic</u> one can get lost in it. There are so many bedrooms on the Second Floor the children are free to urinate in their beds and then jump into another.[25] The pageant princess, with dyed blonde hair and lipstick, and what happened to her, and how she ended up <u>dead in the family basement</u>, is perhaps the most simultaneously credible and ridiculous aspect of all. Although we're saddened by what happened to the real little girl, are we able to separate the real little girl from the Christmas Star?

When we look at the Ramseys, on the surface they seem credible, even eminent. The patriarch is handsome and quietly brimming with intelligence, especially business acumen. The matriarch is beautiful and determined, and sparkling with the charm that got her crowned <u>Miss West Virginia at age 20 in 1977</u>. The children are both cute as a button, and glittering reflections of their parents. And the historic gingerbread mansion, its pathway festooned with Christmas candy canes, a Santa on a sleigh beckoning strangers, appears to be something out of the All-American fairy tale. Not by accident, by design. All the people in this family, including the nannies, participated in some way in setting up the pageantry of the Perfect Family.

But look a little closer, and the Christmas tree isn't real, some of the lights don't work, some of the Christmas gifts are dented or the wrapping torn. The torn wrapping is a symptom of *insatiable appetites* barely held in check. The basement overflows with clutter, and none of the beds are ever made by those who sleep in them. This is a restless family rather than one that sleeps. This is a family where excrement doesn't reside in toilets, but on walls, doors, bedsheets and doctor's notes. The residue of a terminal illness sits on the walls, and the stairs, like <u>an invisible Gargoyle escaped</u> from the *Notre Dame*.

And yet we seem incapable of seeing the other dimension fully. We're so attuned to seeing the Christmas Star that it seems our eyes must continually adjust to the unseen world hidden beneath it. In true crime, of course, this is all we see if we are true True Crime Rocket Scientists.

And so, the important thing around the Ransom Note is less the note itself than the pageantry around it. Yes the semantics matter.[26] Yes the grammar and the graphology is worth looking at. But the shadow that doesn't want to be seen is less the writer of the Ransom Note than the writer trying to explain her innocent discovery of it, when it was everything but innocent.

What we're about to do is revisit Patsy Ramsey as she *pretends* to discover the note. If Patsy wrote the note, she never *discovered* it. If Patsy wrote the note, it means she wrote it to protect someone. And if Patsy wrote the note, and Patsy wrote it to protect someone, then John was aware of and part of the pageantry too, wasn't he? If the Ramsey Ransom note is fake, then the whole thing was an elaborate pageant in which not one but several participated.

So the pageantry doesn't only begin or end with the note. The note is surface light. It's the Christmas Star writ large. The pageantry begins around, on the periphery of the note as well. If there's surface light, there's surface darkness too. Let's deal with that now.

It's March 27, 2000, 21:00 Eastern Time. Patsy's on *CNN*, sitting across from Larry King. She's on a television stage to market her book with her husband. That's the surface light. But Larry's not asking her much about the book. Instead he's asking Patsy questions about polygraph tests that never happened, and questions about *taking* a polygraph that the Ramseys say they were never asked. And then <u>Larry asks Patsy about the ruse of finding the note</u>. This is the shadowy periphery around the note we want to get at.

KING: *Let's go back to that night. It's December 26th, the day after Christmas, right? That's when this occurred.*

JOHN: *Yes.*

KING: *What happened that day?*

JOHN: *December 26th? We were planning to leave for Charlevoix which is – we have a summer cottage up there, we did have.*

<u>KING</u>: *What happened that night? [John flicks his tongue between his lips]. What's the first thing you remember, Patsy?*

<u>PATSY</u>: *The first thing I remember [shaking head] is <u>waking up</u>, getting dressed hurriedly, going downstairs, and putting a few things together to pack to take on the plane.*

That part isn't true. Patsy didn't wake up or get dressed, and she didn't dress hurriedly because she never got undressed. The part to appreciate though isn't the Ransom Note. It's not the handwriting or what's in the note, it's the *woods*. So we don't want to pay attention to the truthfulness of what Patsy's saying here, or lack of. Rather, we want to see where she's steering the story.

When Larry asks her what's the first thing you remember, where Patsy wants to take us – her audience – is to the Random Note. She wants to literally take us by the hand and lead us to the note. It's there for the reason – to distract. And so it's no surprise that the first thing Patsy does, the first thing she "remembers" involves leading us to the prime pageantry device.

KING: *This is about what time?*

<u>PATSY</u> [Shaking her head]: *It's early morning, before daylight.*

KING: *You're up?*

JOHN: *Mmhm.*

PATSY [Licks her lips]: *Mmhm.*

KING: *Then what happens?*

PATSY: *Then I go down the spiral staircase, and [shakes head]...there on one of the runs of the stair is the three-page ransom note.*

And so this is where Patsy wants to take the question "what happened that day" or "what do you remember?" By handing over the Ransom Note, Patsy and John are no longer on the spot, and neither is Burke. Whether you believe in the note or not, you're caught up in the mythos, and the light is more dazzling than the shadow.

KING: *And no one has entered the house. The door isn't open. You read the note.*

<u>PATSY</u> [Slyly interrupting Larry, smiles broadly]: *I don't know that. [That a door isn't open, or that no one has entered the house].*

It's interesting because the moment she discovers a note left by a band of foreign terrorists, Patsy doesn't worry how the note got inside the house, or whether someone got in and took something. The note is simply an enigma. It's not supposed to make sense, and it's not supposed to go anywhere. It's supposed to take you into it, and from there into infinite and unresolvable introspection.

KING: *What did you do?*

<u>PATSY</u>: *Well, I hardly read it, you know, [waves hand over the desk, roleplaying, takes her hands off the table] and didn't take long to understand what was happening. And I ran back upstairs and pushed open her bedroom door, and she was gone.*

Although Patsy has all the time in the world, in this fictitious scenario – it's dark, she's alone, none of the children are awake, she hasn't started cooking anything or doing anything else – she elects to be in a hurry to read. Patsy and John are both readers. They both had piles of paperbacks beside their beds. But a Ransom Note they don't read. They don't have time [even though the note says a call will take place between two and four hours later].

Patsy reveals in her response to the note that she doesn't place much stock in it. She reads it quickly, and apparently not to completion before following just one of the instructions highlighted in it.

We have your daughter.

The rush to JonBenét's bedroom to check whether she's there or not is also pageantry, as – just as unlikely – is the idea of JonBenét having slept in her bed in her bedroom in the first place.

In this subtle nod to the point of the note [jumping effectively to *We have your daughter* which is code for *JonBenét's gone,* which is code for *JonBenét's dead*] we see psychological acknowledgement of the Ramseys overall capacity for neglect. In an apparently life-and-death situation, they don't read the instructions given to them, in fact they ignore them. While this is par for the course for them, we're not sure whether their dismissive attitude to the note is a sign of intellect or something else brooding in the ether. [It's a bit of both].

KING: *Did you think – you knew it was her by the note, right?*

PATSY: *Well, it said "your daughter."*

KING: *You were not concerned about Burke? Did you check Burke?*

PATSY: *Yes.*

JOHN: *We checked him fairly quickly.*

KING: *You brought the note to John?*

But of course Patsy didn't. Because Patsy didn't handle the note. And that's the tricky part here. After writing the note, the note was left on the spiral staircase for the cops to discover, but because they're in the house – within the contrived pageantry – **they now have to participate within and without the periphery of their own construction and reconstruction.** Does that make sense?

And so how does Patsy answer Larry's oh-so-simple question about the note. Did she take it to John? Of course she had to! But she didn't. She left it lying on the floor. And so this is the first moment where Patsy gets a little stuck.

PATSY [Holding both her hands up, palms facing the camera, in response to the question about taking the note to John] : *I don't remember, I tell you. You just – you know, that morning is so chaotic.*

KING [In disbelief]: *You don't remember how you got the note? You don't?*

In a few minutes Larry has gone from a credible scenario to a ridiculous one.

PATSY: *I don't remember exactly, but...*

JOHN [Defensive]: *Well, it was – it was...*

PATSY [Breaking in, throws her hands around]: *I started screaming, "There's a note!" you know?*

By screaming about the note, Patsy doesn't have to take it anywhere. She can effectively transmit her message about the note from anywhere in the house by screaming. Still, it would make sense to pick it up. Do any neighbors hear screaming that morning? Unlikely. Wouldn't the Ramseys want to be quiet so as not to attract the attention of nosy neighbors, particularly on a compromising night like this? So the screaming is also pageantry.

KING: *And you look in JonBenét's room. She's not there. What's the first thing you do?*

JOHN: *Larry, we don't remember. This is three years ago. We've been through this a hundred times.*

KING [Being practical]: *You wrote a book about it, so, I mean, you must have said...*

JOHN: *We outlined it in the book.*

When we cut back through the transcript to Patsy's description of finding the note, this is what we're actually left with.

Then I go down the spiral staircase, and there on one of the runs of the stair is the three-page ransom note. Well, I hurriedly read it, you know, and didn't take long to understand what was happening. And I ran back upstairs.

She doesn't mention screaming or shouting here, but the part we really want to fathom is why Patsy needs to **hardly read the note and then run away from it.** On *CNN* in January 1ˢᵗ, <u>Patsy had said the note didn't make any sense</u>, that it just wasn't registering. But more than three years later, that's changed to "it didn't take long to understand..."

The pageantry of the note itself pales in comparison to the pageantry around the note,[27] just as the pageantry of Christmas [the occasion when it happens] pales in comparison to the endless pageantry leading up to it. The repeated exhortations to have a Merry Christmas before Christmas is actually upon us, the ritual of shopping, wrapping, cooking and dressing up a home and oneself – including the millions who take on the role of an overweight grandpa in a red suit and beard bearing gifts for the world, but too pressed for time to stick around for a chat. Drop the gifts and run is the name of the game.

In the same way the bow on JonBenét's hair shouldn't merely be seen for what it is, but what led up to and around it. Not for what did happen but for what should have, but didn't.

All who celebrate Christmas participate, in one way or another, in the Pageantry around the Christmas Tree. Christmas itself is a spectacle – warm and fuzzy, bright, garish at times, sparkling with tinsel, twinkling stars, sweet Christmas puddings and jingling bells.

One can go so far as to say life itself is pageantry, or as Laurence Overmire, author of *A Revolutionary American Family: The McDonalds of Somerset County, New Jersey* puts it:

"All of us are part of a beautiful pageantry of human experience. Let us make the most of this life in all we do."

What Overmire's getting at here is the charming if naïve frivolity we humans engage in in spite of the looming certainty of death. It's a little like celebrating Christmas one day knowing with absolute certainty you and your family are headed to Auschwitz the next. Given that perspective, does one ramp up the pageantry or subdue it? It's the question of the ages. How are we to treat life given its crushing finitude?

What does it mean to do exactly as Overmire asks; what does it mean to *make the most of this life*?

The Pageantry of the Christmas Tree encourages us to appreciate the surface layer of things. Even if trees aren't real, or the bearer of gifts a modern fiction [or in the Ramseys' case, a suspect][28], all that matters is that the family enjoy a safe and secure celebration of materialism – again, in a finite world that of late has started running a serious fever. A child could tell you that climate change is real, but we'd prefer to continue with the everyday pageantry as if it's not, as if there's no tomorrow.

This psychology is a battle between surface things versus things unseen. That's another question of the ages. Should women align themselves with men who have obvious cauldrons of gold scattered about their thrones, and should men, in turn, accumulate pots of gold to ensnare the best women – the best women being the most superficially attractive. Thin. Fit. Good hair. Nice tits?

Or should we align ourselves with the surface things and the things unseen, and especially the things unseen [in ourselves and in others]. Unseen things matter more than seen things. Honesty, loyalty, integrity and commitment mean far more than the most beautiful human being who is flagrantly dishonest, disloyal and deceitful. And yet our world as it's presently configured, doesn't seem to care. It cares more about pageantry than reality.

The question the Ramsey Christmas Star quietly asks is whether we see the surface light or surface darkness? Can we see what's inside versus what's on the surface? The analogy goes further in that the pile of wrapped gifts under the tree can only be utilized if torn open. Something can only be consumed by destroying its outer wrapping. Is the same true of us?

Being Beautiful in the 21st Century

Lee Chandler: *I can't beat it. I can't beat it. I'm sorry.* — Manchester by the Sea

Just as there is the pageantry of the note, and the pageantry around the note, there is the pageantry of the polygraphs, and the pageantry around the polygraphs. When the esteemed polygrapher Edward Gelb, a former president of the American Polygraph Association asked Patsy whether the handwriting on the Ransom Note found in the home was hers, Patsy said no. According to the *Daily Camera*:

"Based on the numerical scoring of the examinations in this series, Patsy Ramsey was telling the truth when she denied writing the JonBenét ransom note."

Pageantry is part and parcel of our society. Pageantry changes outcomes. Pageantry works. Pageantry – one could argue – is reality. And reality, arguably, is pageantry. The reality of True Crime Rocket Science however is *not* pageantry.

23 years after JonBenét's murder we're faced with some uncomfortable echoes from that little girl's brief time under the Colorado sun. In her last days JonBenét struggled to sleep. She struggled with insomnia. We live in a world where sleep apnoea is rife; where almost everyone – seemingly – has serious difficulty switching off from the billowing forests of restless pageantry.

If the Ramseys didn't involve themselves in their children's urine, do we – in the 21st century – care about the urine of our time? Coal emissions? Social Media addiction? Obesity? Or do we allow someone else to take care of it? Isn't that what being beautiful in the 21st century is all about? Stepping up on stage for a pageant, receiving applause and then returning home to insomnia and urinating in our beds?

It's ignominious, the intimacy of urine in the Ramsey story, to the innocence and destruction of JonBenét. One feels somehow if the bedwetting had been acknowledged and dealt with, perhaps everything else would have been taken care of. But there's the rub. One has to care to take care of. According to Linda Hoffman-Pugh, during the summer of 1996:

*"JonBenét started wearing those diaper type underpants-Pull-Ups. She even wore them to bed. **There was always a wet one in the trash.** By the end of the summer, Patsy was trying to get her to do without them. Then JonBenét started wetting the bed again. **Almost every day I was there, there was a wet bed.** Patsy said she wasn't going to use Pull-Ups again. **She just put a plastic cover on the bed.** No big deal to her. By the time I'd come in the morning, Patsy would have all the sheets off the bed and in the laundry. JonBenét's white blanket would already be in the dryer. The Ramseys had two washer-dryers-one in the basement and a stackable unit in a closet just outside JonBenét's room."*

Patsy's attitude seemed less to deal with the situation than to clean it, or have someone else deal with it, or otherwise get rid of it. The other housekeeper had a similar impression of John.

<u>WILCOX:</u> *When John says to the camera, "I didn't know she wet the bed, or not very much." I happen to know myself, he walked upstairs, [if] she had wet her bed, I came in on a Monday morning and he said, "Could you change her bed? **She's wet it again."***

If John and Patsy knew their children were chronic bedwetters, and the housekeepers seem to confirm they did know, and they did nothing about it for years, then weren't they culpable of neglect, or is chronic bedwetting exempt from that category? What do you think? Back to the housekeeper.

WILCOX: *The thing that strikes me as odd, I knew JonBenét between two-and-a-half and four [years old]. During that time, JonBenét did wet the bed but it wasn't chronic. It was every now and then.* **But, it got progressively worse.**

Why was the bedwetting getting worse? Well, wasn't it the same reason the little dog got sick and disappeared? The neglect didn't improve over time, it worsened.

WILCOX: *I would think that a six-year-old would wet the bed less than a four-year-old or a two-year-old.* **It actually got worse...**[And] *both her and Burke both wet the bed. Burke was seven-years-old and he also wet the bed. I didn't think it was odd at the time, because it sometimes runs in families and it's more common in boys.*

When we cast back at Patsy and see how a former beauty queen raised her daughter to be beautiful only to be murdered, and for her parents to face a lifetime of suspicion and – arguably – shame, it begs the question: Do we know any more what beauty is?

For all Patsy's valiant or villainous efforts to defend herself or defeat the inquiries into herself, she succumbed to cancer in 2006, after going into remission in 2002. Ten years after JonBenét was dead, Patsy was dead too. Do we know any more what beauty is? Do we know what to do with, or how to take care of it? To address this question let's examine three different women.

1.   Viktoria Odintcova and the Skyscraper Stunt

At the 2017 Grammy Awards, various female icons stepped in front of the paparazzi to interpret their version of beauty. It varied from

Lady Gaga's on the chin attention pleading vulgarity, Heidi Klum's silvery simplicity, blue banality, maroon madness, from the sublime to the silly, from Beyoncé's gaudy gold to Katy Perry's ridiculousness. How much of it was beautiful to begin with?

Do we know any more what beauty is?

What does it mean to be beautiful in the 21st century?

Is it possible to be beautiful without being on social media, without having an audience to show you are, or them saying you are?

In 2017, an American high school student took to social media to criticize her school for shaming her wardrobe choice on civvies day. In this "post-truth" society, what are the standards for appropriate and inappropriate? We don't seem to know any more what it means to be beautiful.

When a beautiful woman must resort to risking her life simply to attract attention, something has gone wrong with the world, and with her.

From *Yahoo*:

A video of Viktoria Odintcova dangling off the ledge of a 73-story building in the United Arab Emirates recently went viral. Why did she do it? For a good photo (and attention, of course)…Odintcova grips a blond helper's hand as he confidently encourages her to lean away from the top of the 1,000-foot building. As she leans back, her hair flows and her eyes close, and somehow she gets comfortable enough to look serene in images captured by her team.

As if that were not enough of a risk, she then gets down on her knees, while still holding the hand of her "spotter" and then gracefully flops off the rails, the guy's forearm strength the only thing keeping her from plum-meting to the ground. Somehow, she still looks beautiful, with her T-shirt falling off her shoulders, and her sneakers…kicking about as if she's just dangling from the side of a pool. She lived to share the tale, and has been retelling it to her 3.3 million Instagram followers.

Is this what being beautiful means in the 21st century? Pageantry from the top of a 1,000 foot building – or nothing?

2.   Qandeel Baloch, Pakistan's social media star and "Family Honor"

Even marketers, who reflect, shape, or try to influence society's views on beauty, <u>sometimes get it completely wrong</u>. Beauty today can be bought. Pageantry is the opposite of grief. Pageantry is shallow, meaningless and fickle. Its value may be as deep as a mood swing or a sample sip of something; tasted but instantly forgotten. All of social media is pageantry and all of it is forgettable. Our ardent archive of likes and retweets are forgotten the moment we execute them.

And yet if we think our attitudes to beauty [which are really our attitudes to each other's surfaces] have no consequences, in fact, they do. Just as surface stuff impacted deeper stuff in the Ramsey case with lifelong consequences, the same applies in the rest of the world. Take Qandeel Baloch, Pakistan's social media star for instance.

From *CNN*:

The brother of Pakistani social media star, Qandeel Baloch, who ex-pressed pride for having killed his sister, has been charged with a crime against the state for the so-called "honor" killing… Waseem Baloch… confessed to killing one of Pakistan's most famous and controversial on-line celebrities because "girls are born to stay home.

A new provision was inserted into Pakistan's penal code making it illegal to kill someone even if the parents of the victim approve.

Previously the provision read that if the parents approved of the killing of their child, it was seen by the law to be legal. Ring a bell?

Back to *CNN*:

"Under Islamic law, murder is seen as a forgivable act..." The 25 year-old Qandeel was strangled Friday at her family home in the city of Multan in the Pakistani province of Punjab. After going on the run, her brother was later arrested. In his confession video, he expresses no regret. "I am proud of what I did. I drugged her first, then I killed her," Waseem Baloch says. "She was bringing dishonor to our family."

No dipshit, it wasn't dishonour, it was pure kindergarten jealousy. If the Qandeel Baloch case angers us it should. But even more than anger, we should feel grief. The inner child of this world appears to have died a long time ago, and what remains is a shell, covered and re-covered in gaudy artwork as if it makes up for the hollow vacuum within.

Our attitudes to beauty are our attitudes to ourselves, and our own worth. They have real lifelong consequences, but what does that mean? What does it mean to absorb the world's cruel gaze as a sort of light of revelation into our lives? What happens when we don't filter that invasive radioactive light, cutting through everything like X-rays, and showing the world's skeletons inside every closet?

3. Katelyn Nicole Davis Broadcasts her Suicide Live – and everyone watches

What does it mean to accept surface definitions of who we are and fully internalize them? What does it mean to evaluate ourselves as little more than beautiful or ugly lies, but still lies? Is it harmless? Is it harmless to accept the world's mutable verdict of ourselves above our own?

From *News24*:

Video of a 12-year-old US girl's suicide **broadcast live** has gone viral around the world, and local police say they're unable to do anything *about it. Katelyn Nicole Davis of Cedartown in northern Georgia posted the 40-minute video on December 30 showing her placing her phone in her front yard, tying a rope around a tree limb and saying goodbye to her family and friends in front of the camera.*

"I'm sorry that I'm not pretty enough," she says in tears, carefully made up and dressed in a white blouse and jeans. "I'm sorry for everything. I'm really, truly sorry. But I can't do this."

The video is very, very difficult to watch, and I'm not referring to the suicide [which I haven't watched]. Where Katelyn is openly crying and openly apologizing for not being good enough, one can feel the raw emotion like razor cuts on the heart. Every word tears at the heartstrings. You can feel Katelyn's anguish, and one feels a desperate wish rising in one's chest to reach out to her and soothe her. But in the twelve-year-old's space, she's inconsolable.

From *News24*:

The video then shows her tying the rope around her neck and hanging herself. Davis had said in another video several days before her death that she had been sexually abused by a family member, the local Rome News-Tribune newspaper reported. Although Davis's family deleted a page with the video depicting her suicide from her Facebook profile, it has been widely shared on YouTube and other websites around the world.

Katelyn's video of her death[29] is an inversion of Viktoria Odintcova skyscraper stunt. Rather than defy death to get attention, to have her worth acknowledged [via page views], Katelyn has accepted her version of society's cynical view of her [based on her perceived appearance]. At twelve years old! She then carries out the sentence she imputes to herself, and broadcasts it almost as a final duty to the same society that condemned her. That social media *machine society* is not a living or loving society; it's bristling with avarice, able to treat people as nothing more than machine code in machine mainframes.

We live in a society where a twelve-year-old's death is reported *because of a video* being harmful to other kids, rather than the police investigating what harmed this child. That's how heartless it's become.

According to psychcentral.com:

*The problem is **a society that has so few social resources available to its poor and those most in emotional need that a 12 year old feels her only choice is to end her own life.***

From what I've been able to piece together, Katelyn lived in a crowded pigsty with drug addicts in minimal privacy and was so chronically neglected, she had to sleep on a sodden mattress on the floor besides a broken pipe. In winter.

Katelyn and her younger sister appear to have been sexually abused by her mother's string of dodgy boyfriends. Drugs form a background to the absolute decay not only of the physical integrity of the home, but the physical bodies of those living inside it.

What is beauty in the 21st century? We are a society plagued with neglect. Empty-hearted people are everywhere pretending to be stars while concealing their true, shadowy selves. Excess begets emptiness. Emptiness begets numbness. Numbness begets a kind of wound that never heals unless we can learn to grieve and then heal from our grief. You can't heal from what you don't acknowledge

And so instead of healing we're hollering. Everyone hollering on their platforms, but no one really has anything to say. Empty barrels filled with a profound darkness make a great clamour signifying nothing. The drug addicted life is precisely that, but you don't need drugs to be poisoned, any addiction will do.

We are a society nourishing ourselves on cocktails laced with poison. <u>Our families have become poisoned, our spouses, our children.</u> We all see it, we all know it, but <u>we drink it anyway.</u>

Listen. Listen carefully.

Look. Look carefully.

<u>Katelyn's wearing a pink sequin star sewn onto a black shirt.</u> The pageantry of social media is no escape from the giant, dripping black maw gaping over the small flickering candle. Where then do broken people of this world find refuge?

In a world without justice, where can the just turn to for asylum?

Douglas' Ducks in a Row?

"When the Spin Portion of last night's A&E program started, I had to turn off the TV to save my sanity."
— chemgirl on websleuths.com

On January 28th, 1997, just over a month after JonBenét's murder, Ex-FBI profiler John Douglas gave an extensive interview to NBC's *Dateline*[30] about his world-leading insights into the Ramsey case, and into John and Patsy in particular.

Based on his book *Law & Disorder*, Douglas said he was informed about the Ramsey situation on Monday, January 6th, 1997 – barely a week after the Ramseys interview with Cabell on *CNN*. By then the Ramseys hadn't spoken to any other media, or the cops. Team Ramsey, however, was looking for a credible expert to hire. They wanted John to talk to an expert at length and have this expert sing John's praises to the media.

So Team Ramsey went through a list of retired FBI agents. They called a colleague of Douglas' who turned them down. When they called Douglas he accepted.

He's not explicit about times and dates in his book, but reading between the lines it appears Douglas made the trip from Provo, Utah to Denver Colorado two days after he received the message – he says – on his answering machine from a Denver-based private detective.[31]

On Wednesday, January 8th Douglas arrived in Boulder by aircraft, then headed straight from the airport in Denver to the offices of the Ramseys' lawyers at the time, Lee Foreman and Bryan Morgan.

According to Douglas he had a few initial misconceptions about the Ramsey crime scene which Team Ramsey quickly straightened out for him. His second misconception[32] was that there had been a "considerable delay" in contacting law enforcement after Patsy had discovered the Ransom Note. The lawyers were quick to point out that this wasn't the case, in fact despite warnings not to contact the authorities in the note, the Ramseys did so immediately.

We won't go into the breathless "Hurry! Hurry! Hurry!" pageantry of the emergency call itself in this narrative, except to be clear if the note had been written over a length of time in the home, then not only was writing the letter itself part of the "considerable time" that elapsed following the incident, the note may have been completed closer to midnight, perhaps three or four in the morning.[33] In a scenario where the Ramseys were awake all night covering up, the call *wasn't* made soon after anyone woke up. The 05:52 911 call on the day after Christmas was *timed to suggest someone woke up* and immediately called the cops. In other words, it was pageantry too, wasn't it?

Douglas also acknowledged to Team Ramsey he was under the impression John and Patsy had been stonewalling the cops. Absolutely not, Bryan Morgan told Douglas the Ramseys had been "completely cooperative" [they'd just not actually agreed to be interviewed by the police almost three weeks after the murder].

Douglas apparently took Morgan at his word, accepting that the Ramseys had been happy to open their home to a search and had freely "answered all questions" and provided hair and blood samples. The lawyers who the Ramseys had lawyered up with explained to their new consultant that the Ramseys had only lawyered up because they were being wrongly fingered as suspects. In fact the reverse was closer to the truth. When the Ramseys lawyered up just hours after the incident,[34] *that's* what led to suspicion around their possible involvement.

On the evening of January 8th, the same day as Douglas' arrival, he was rushed to the crime scene. Douglas was told the house had recently been made available for an open-house tour. Uh-oh, Douglas thought.

The next day, Thursday January 9th, 1997, Douglas sat down for four hours with John Ramsey.[35] We don't know whether John told Douglas he had one of his books – *Mindhunter* – in his library, and if he did, how Douglas reacted. If John did tell him, this may have flattered the author, but it may also have indicated to a sober mind the possibility that through that book, the Ramseys had a potential blueprint to cover up a crime scene, and figure out how to avoid capture by literally reading a step-by-step guide. If the Ransom Note is a fake, it feels like Exhibit A not only in pageantry, but also a relatively educated form of pageantry. Its writer wasn't a seasoned cop, but she was no slouch either.[36]

Douglas thought John looked appropriately sad. John then led the former agent through the events, starting with him and Patsy taking photos of the children as they opened their Christmas gifts. Once again, this brings us back to the last photo. Did Douglas ask to see these images? Did Douglas get to see the image that's just been released? Did he compare the post mortem and autopsy photos to the actual last photo, and if so, did he draw any conclusions? If he didn't then, has he since?

In John's account to Douglas, when they returned from the Whites, JonBenét was asleep and had to be carried inside and put in bed.

Let's go to the *Dateline* clip to pick up Douglas' exact version on this that aspect.

REPORTER: *The Ramseys told Douglas that they all went to bed very early Christmas night, because they were planning to fly to their other home in Michigan, the next morning.*

DOUGLAS: *Mr. Ramsey gets up, takes a shower. The mother gets up, goes downstairs to make some coffee [Douglas waves his hand]. Goes down the spiral staircase. On the last step there's three pages of the... uh...letter. Starts reading it. Doesn't know what it is. Uh and then she starts screaming. Mr Ramsey comes down...and uh [shakes head, licks his lips]... you know, the instructions are [shifts in his seat] don't contact the FBI, don't contact the police.*

What's wrong with this hand-me-down version from John? Not *everyone* went to bed early that night. If Kolar's Pineapple Theory is good for anything, Burke didn't go to bed early. And based on the autopsy results of JonBenét's stomach contents, JonBenét ate pieces of fruit two hours before her death late that night as well.

Douglas isn't completely accurate on Patsy's version here in that he doesn't describe Patsy running upstairs. He is on point by not being explicit on either of the Ramseys handling the note. But this doesn't bother him. He doesn't raise this obvious point as a point of concern. There's a Ransom Note, the most important artefact in the story, and the Ramseys themselves treat it as if it's radioactive, and that's okay. They read it, or speed-read[37] it with their hands behind their backs, then run away from it kicking and screaming. Perfectly normal.

In Lawrence Schiller's book *Perfect Murder Perfect Town*, Pat Korten, Team Ramsey's high-powered PR dude, is quoted at some length. In one instance where Korten refers to the Ramseys hiring Douglas he highlights how "emphatic" Douglas was about "putting some of the Ransom Note" in the public domain. In other words, what Douglas wanted to do Korten wanted to do, and what Korten wanted to do the Ramseys wanted to do. And what the Ramseys wanted was for everyone to pay attention to the damn Ransom Note. And so, everyone did and arguably, we still are. John Ramsey standing in front of a poster-sized mock-up of the note in A&E's documentary in April 2019 shows the ridiculous Ransom Note has done its work – it's stood the test of time. It's distracted attention from the Ramseys *somewhere else*, even if that somewhere else is nowhere in particular.

And even if attention has eventually circled back to Patsy, and it has, it's still circled away from JonBenét's killer. Even if one is focused on Patsy as the writer, it's still a case of being blinded by the *Christmas Star*, and so blinded we're unable to see into the surface darkness illuminated by that star.

In early January, when Douglas flew into Colorado, he arrived to discover the Ramseys were widely regarded as the chief suspects in JonBenét's death. But what if suspicion could be conjured elsewhere through sleight of hand – legal and otherwise? Korten emphasized that what they wanted was for the public to pay attention to the note so that they could then inundate the cops with tips to the "real killer", which is exactly what happened.

REPORTER: *The so-called[38] Ransom Note that was left at the Ramseys home, demands $118 000. And we now know 118 000 is the amount of the bonus…John Ramsey…was expecting this year. What does that say to you?*

DOUGLAS: *Well, who has this knowledge? Uh, the wife doesn't have the knowledge.*

Well, she probably did. Patsy's father, Don Paugh, worked for John as vice president in charge of operations. When the Ramseys moved to Boulder, Don stayed in an apartment in Boulder "maintained by Access Graphics"[39] when it was necessary for him to be in town on Access Graphics-related business.

Besides Don, Patsy's siblings Pam and Polly, and even her mother Nedra[40] were all on the company payroll at one time or another. So in spite of Douglas' view, it was very likely Patsy did know the payroll amounts, and as a result of her intimate knowledge of her husband's business, little wonder Patsy herself may have felt like a cross between a wife and an employee. Besides this, Patsy had helped John set up the business to begin with.

In a scenario where Patsy's dad and other family members worked for her husband, we can clearly see a strong incentive for Patsy to go pageant-crazy if or when a crisis exploded under them in the Ramsey home, as it did on Christmas Night.

And there's something else. Isn't it curious how Douglas in his interview doesn't say Patsy's name. He refers to her once as "the wife" and on another occasion as "the mother." He doesn't refer to John as John either, but as "Mr Ramsey" [just as the somewhat subservient note does]

DOUGLAS: *She doesn't know anything about that…Uh, so…to me…it begins to tell me more about the person who's responsible. This person has very unique, intimate knowledge about his financial workings. Therefore the person [the Ransom Note writer] would have to be…somehow related…to uh…his employment.*

We won't take this further than that, but to be fair, Douglas isn't wrong. Remember what the housekeeper Linda Wilcox said?

*They didn't act like a married couple…**they [seemed like] business associates. She was like his secretary, not his wife.***

When we review Douglas' role as the Ramseys' arch Apologist, we need to move beyond nit-picking the facts from the fiction. Do we really want to be stuck trying to prove whether Patsy wrote the note or not?[41] Or do we want to look beyond the surface light towards the surface darkness?

If the Ransom Note is both credible and ridiculous [and TCRS sees it as more of the latter than the former], then a credible expert who doesn't see the note as ridiculous, feels ridiculous in itself, doesn't it?

In *Perfect Murder Perfect Town* we get a tiny peek through the crack of the colossal egg of ridiculousness that has enveloped this case. Somewhere around March 1997, just before giving a scheduled lecture at Kutztown University in Pennsylvania, Douglas called a press conference. Rumors had been circulating that Patsy's handwriting had not been excluded as a possible author of the Ransom Note. The media wanted to know what Douglas thought about this? Did he want to retract his position on the Ramseys? And what was Douglas' expert opinion on the mother?

Incredibly, Douglas admitted he'd not being asked by Team Ramsey to investigate Patsy, so he hadn't profiled her. None of the lawyers had specifically asked Douglas whether Patsy fit the profile [Douglas' *criteria* as Schiller puts it] for the murderer.[42] And presumably Douglas didn't think to do the same on Burke either.

What matters here is less the tomfoolery and hocus pocus around the note, because the note is ridiculous in itself. What matters are the behaviours and silhouettes of the players around it.

Who steps forward and holds the note up as something credible and authentic and worth paying attention to? A FBI profiler who in the same breath says John's innocent and the note is real. The media were also somewhat complicit in the pageantry, shape shifting and shadow-boxing around how to think about the Ransom Note. On January 14th, 1997 the *Denver Post* described Douglas as "the inspiration for one of the central characters in the movie *Silence of the Lambs*. If Douglas, the former head of the FBI's behavioural science unit in Quantico said John was in the clear, and the note legit, who was anyone to criticize that? Wasn't the Mindhunter supposed to be the best in the business, a leading authority, the brightest star in the cosmos of criminal profiling?

And isn't that what John needed right then, when the media was baying for their blood? For a big gun to silence the clamour by providing expert knowledge that would soon stem the tide rising against them.

A Disturbance in the Guest Bedroom?

"Look, as sentient meat, however illusory our identities are, we craft those identities by making value judgments: everybody judges, all the time."
— Detective Rust Cohle, True Detective, 2014

If JonBenét didn't sleep in her own bed, in her own bedroom, there are not one but two alternatives where she could have slept, that is if sleeping was something she wanted to do.

The obvious first option was <u>the room directly adjacent to her own</u> – John Andrew's bedroom, otherwise known as <u>the guest bedroom</u>. This room on the north-west corner of the house was furthest from Burke's bedroom, and for that matter, the master bedroom upstairs. It was also the room Patsy used while recovering from chemotherapy. This fact is important, because a) the bathroom Patsy would have used during convalescence would have a medical kit, an arsenal at hand to deal with the symptoms of chemotherapy [nausea, vomiting, hair loss] and b) <u>the drawers in the bathroom appear to have been used</u> on the night of the murder by someone familiar with them.

The bed in the guest bedroom was the only double bed on the first floor and the only one besides the one in the master bedroom. This means the guest bedroom was also a more likely place for two children who'd wet their beds to share a bed.

The second option for JonBenét was to sleep in Burke's bedroom on the spare bed there. The question is which is more likely: that JonBenét would leave her room to sleep in Burke's room, or would Burke leave his room to sleep in JonBenét's [or John Andrew's room]?

Now although John Ramsey let slip on *CNN* on January 1st 1997 that "sometimes" JonBenét would ⊠sleep in there⊠ [in Burke's room], it may well be that the opposite was true. When Dan Schuler interviewed Burke, Burke claimed when his bed was cold he would sleep somewhere else besides his bedroom, or the other bed in his bedroom.

SCHULER [Referring to JonBenét's bedroom]: *This bedroom?*

BURKE: *I would sometimes sleep on…I forget which bed. But I would sometimes sleep in there 'cause mine got cold.*

Cold could be a reference to the discomfort of a wet bed, especially in winter.

SCHULER [Pressing]: *'Cause your room got cold. So whose bed was this?*

BURKE: *JonBenét.*

We ought to be careful making assumptions. Going by the letter of the transcript it sounds like Burke was pointing to beds in an image, when he was really pointing out JonBenét bedroom. Once again we shouldn't blinded by the details, or the bright light of the star. We need to acknowledge the shadow underneath it, and that shadow is this:

I would sometimes sleep in JonBenét's room…

What this reveals is a willingness from Burke to leave his room – possibly frequently, possibly not – and enter JonBenét's room. The grapefruit-sized turd left on JonBenét's sheets suggests more than a passing familiarity with JonBenét's quarters. But we also have two additional dimensions to the musical beds going on. Both children are bedwetters, and Burke emphasizes that he left his bed particularly when it was cold. Well, Christmas was about the coldest time of the year.

We won't take this any further, because we want to deal with the guest bedroom, but there's a final box to check in this area of cold beds, cold bedrooms and cold nights. It comes from the very next section of the transcript.

SCHULER: *Okay, so when it gets real cold in the winter, <u>would you sleep over here?</u> [Pointing to JonBenét's bedroom].*

BURKE: *Yeah. I would sleep in there 'cause my room's kind of an older part of the house.*

That's true. In fact <u>the three tall, vertical windows in Burke's bedroom [opposite his bed]</u> are part of the historic gable facing the front garden and road. For all these years photos of the house have focused – perhaps without knowing it – on Burke's room and the window peeking out of the ground directly below it, the basement window.

SCHULER: *…without the insulation in them. Okay, how often would you sleep over here sometimes?*

BURKE: *Usually like really cold nights.*[43]

We know that trace snow fell that night, on the day after Christmas, so that night was clearly <u>one of Burke's *really cold nights*</u>. It's unclear whether Schuler asked Burke where he slept on the night in question,[44] but it's clear where drawing the obvious inference in this regard takes us.

Detective Lou Smit was fixated on the guest bedroom. He believed it was the likeliest spot for <u>an intruder intent on stalking JonBenét</u> to hide out until she arrived home. Smit reinforced his support for the guest bedroom by pointing out that the bedding on JonBenét's bed wasn't wet or urine-stained. And a sack of rope was discovered in the guest bedroom which the Ramseys said they couldn't explain.[45] We don't know whether Burke's was, but we do know <u>Burke's bed was made</u> – unusually – <u>by none other than John Ramsey himself</u>, and further, that JonBenét's clothing was urine-stained, perhaps after she suffered the fatal blow. But regardless of when JonBenét suffered the fatal blow, the question is where she was when it happened, and what happened to the urine underneath her.

James Kolar is of the belief that the urine stains on the carpet in front of the wine cellar door point to the area where JonBenét died. This doesn't make any sense. Why would anyone murder someone <u>at the end of a passage</u> *in front of a door* and not behind it?[46]

Kolar's theory isn't completely nonsensical however, because a child wouldn't necessarily be able to reach <u>the locking mechanism above the door</u>. On the other hand, if JonBenét died somewhere else, one imagines if she was carried from some other location, she was likely placed on the ground in order to reach the latch above the door. One imagines it requires both an unlatching of the latch above and opening the doorknob.

More support for Kolar's theory is that <u>Patsy's paint tray was found on the carpet</u> on the ground close to the door. So doesn't it make sense that someone sat there, on the ground, and fashioned a garrotte? No it does not. JonBenét's body was hidden *behind* the door, so it stands to reason that whoever sexually interfered with and murdered JonBenét would <u>*not have done so in plain sight*</u> *in front of the door* at the end of the passage. Besides this, a fragment of wood missing from the paintbrush [a piece Smit believes was inserted in JonBenét's vagina[47]] was never found. This too suggests things in the basement weren't as they seemed either.

The Ramsey crime scene is an elaborately staged crime scene. The only question is how elaborate. The Ransom Note suggests the staging is far more elaborate than it appears. Just the three pages of the Ransom Note indicate a heck of a lot of afterthought went into the staging, and theoretically there was plenty of time to do it. The fact that there was a practise note as well suggests not only afterthought, but forethought to the staging as well. The suitcase propped below the broken basement window, along with the smear on the wall, is also part of a flowery attempt at crime scene staging.

What feels unique in the staging of the Ramsey home is the abundance of not only afterthought, but forethought as well. Think about how someone is prepared for a pageant after a previous pageant, but also using the knowledge from previous competitions to improve on the next one. What we mean in the context of the Ramsey case is that prior to staging, the staging and the scene is given *due consideration*. It's not just staging after the fact. So, to illustrate, prior to writing the actual Ransom Note its author had to decide who to address it to, what the note was going to say, what sort of tone and identity the fictional author would take etc. There was also the practical issue of how to disguise or at least camouflage the handwriting.[48] All of this formed the forethought prior to the execution.

The guest bedroom certainly provides an interesting area in which to test this hypothesis. Is the guest bedroom staged? The fact that a suitcase is used to stage the exit of the phantom intruder feeds into the psychology of suitcases. The family was planning a trip and Patsy had suitcases on her mind. The suitcase then became part of the *schema* of staging. The suitcase was also John Andrew's, which *suggests* it came from John Andrew's room [though not necessarily], and the movement of a suitcase from upstairs to downstairs, to misdirect attention away from _that_ room [and who was in that room] to misdirecting attention away from another room [and who is in _that_ room] in the basement is a double mirror for the practise and real Ransom Note, both of which are fake.

The suitcase is a *second ransom note* in that it takes the fiction of the Ransom Note and manifests it into physical reality. The broken window, the open window and the suitcase basically form a trifecta saying *Intruder Alert*. The Ransom Note provides a psychological primer for it rather than a guide map. None of this is rocket science because all of it is the blinding *Christmas Star*. What's the shadowy behemoth under it? Well, isn't the suitcase and painting tray taken from the guest room to take attention out of that room? And isn't the suitcase, painting tray and broken window meant to take attention into those rooms and spaces?

The suitcase with a pile of clothes on the bed seems to say *packing went on here* just as the suitcase in the basement seems to say *Intruder Alert Here*. If packing was going on on that bed it was a ridiculous mess – where are all the other suitcases? Where are everyone else's clothes? Shouldn't there be four sets of clothes on the bed if the bed is Ground Zero for luggage? But why would Patsy choose a room furthest from her own, and John's, and Burke's, to pack? And why wouldn't she simply leave packing for the next morning? Wouldn't that be more Patsy's style, and the family's style? Isn't that what neglectful parents and disobedient children do – leave things until the last moment [including going to bed]. And isn't that why Patsy set the alarm for 05:30?

If the room was being used to pack and collect clothing, then it makes sense that both Burke and JonBenét were summoned to it on that fateful night; perhaps they were asked to collect some of their favorite items of clothing and leave it on the bed. It also makes sense that one or both children might have carried their new toys with them, and perhaps lingered in the room while Patsy packed or after Patsy left.[49]

But what about the paint tray?

Since Patsy spent extended time convalescing in John Andrew's room, it's certainly possible much of this sojourn in the north-western wing of the house may also have included painting. What else does one do when one's bedridden? If true, then when Patsy recovered, she may not have transferred her painting supplies from upstairs to downstairs. Thus, the paint tray may have originally been in the guest bedroom as well.

The late transfer of suitcase, paint tray and JonBenét's body speaks about the same delayed attending to of everything else. *Everything was put off.* If there was bedwetting, it was put off. If Burke was smearing crap, they'd deal with that later. If someone made a mess, the house-keepers would pick it up, or wash it up eventually. If Patsy got cancer, she'd put that behind her too. If JonBenét was getting a bike Burke would get his the following month. If something happened to JonBenét, a Ransom Note might *put off* the investigation for a while.

When JonBenét was found dead, this psychology appears to have turned on its head. From putting off it became *putting on.* If the packing was put off, now – with attention about to be laser-focused on them – clothes and a suitcase were *put on* the bed to make it look like they were a family on top of everything. And certain things that were usually put on were *put off.* Instead of *putting on* a new outfit that day, Patsy stayed in her old one, a massive *faux pas* for a former Miss Virginia but then – perhaps – it was because she was about to put on the best pageant[50] of her life.

Christmas Star

"Don't be afraid of who you are." – Princess Leia,
Star Wars The Rise of Skywalker

Is it possible after 23 years to see the same thing with different eyes? We know it's possible to see the same thing for 23 years, and that it's possible to never stop seeing the same thing, but are we capable of *seeing the unseen*? Can we actually train our eyes to adjust to and see the shadow instead of the light? Of course we can.

We may be wired to see the lights, just as we're wired to respond to stimulus rather than a lack of stimulus. True crime and staged crime scenes tend to be about removing the stimulus and then waving a misdirecting flag at something else. Nowhere is this more the case in a crime scene than in this one.

The flags of misdirection in the Ramsey case are many. Besides the Ransom Note, what is there to look at? What about the thing that's more obvious even than the Ransom Note – the children at the center of this story sitting under the Christmas tree. Let's focus on that in this final chapter, shall we?

Take a close look at the snaps of JonBenét below the Christmas tree, and beside her brother Burke on that final Christmas morning unwrapping gifts and strutting on the carpet to tear open another present. JonBenét appears full of spark, doesn't she?[51] But that same spark that we know so well is somehow lacking in <u>the expressionless black and white tones of the last photo</u>. Why is that? Was she simply caught off guard, or is the last photo an illustration of JonBenét always being reminded to be on her guard for the camera? And isn't that why photos like this where she appears subdued and even sad are rare to non-existent? Because that side was always deliberately put aside, or deliberately hidden.

Whether it's smiling sweetly <u>with her mother</u>, or <u>crowing loudly and exuberantly</u> in triumph about her brand new green bicycle, the Jon-Benét in the last photo *isn't* <u>the JonBenét we feel we've gotten to know all these years</u>. There's a weariness in the eyes, a pallor, perhaps even a jaundice to her face. For once a smile is missing from her mouth. In each of <u>the final photos of JonBenét</u> there's invariably <u>a wide, toothy grin</u>. Not in this one.

It's just not <u>the JonBenét we know</u>. It's some other JonBenét, isn't it?

One doesn't have to be a rocket scientist to see that there's been another JonBenét all along, just as there's been another Burke, another Patsy, another John and even another Jacques-the-dog. There's also the practise ransom note.

When JonBenét wasn't on stage doing pageants, she was a child with a sleep disorder, a TV addict and a bed wetter with an appetite for pineapple. In this respect [the pageants and the bedwetting in combination] JonBenét was an unusual little girl.

When Burke wasn't playing baseball or doing his thing as an eagle scout, <u>if Linda Hoffman-Pugh's account is to be believed</u>, he was playing with his poop, including sculpting it into grapefruit-sized balls. In Patsy's case there was cancer. In John's case, there were rumors of <u>another affair</u>.[52]

But it's not necessary that we know any of this stuff. We don't have to connect Burke's swing with a golf club, or <u>Dr. Bernhard's sip from</u>

Burke's soda, or go through the children's medical records in search of patterns of scatological behaviour or sexual contact. _This_ is sufficient. All we need to know is before she went to bed on Christmas Night JonBenét had this bow in her hair, and when she was found at around 13:00 the next morning [with a cracked skull, strangled to death and sexually interfered with] that bow was still in her hair.

The brown, black and white bow is both the _Christmas Star_ and the tree underneath supporting it in the darkness. The star of the bow speaks candidly of a child who didn't go to bed that night, who wasn't asleep, who wasn't tucked into bed and who was hungry enough to still be eating pineapple later that night. No one changed her clothes. Nobody read her a bedtime story.[53]

The bow also speaks of the shadowy tree underneath the star, supporting it in the darkness. The bow speaks of a child found in the darkness and then hidden in an even darker place. She was then left on the floor, the light turned off and the door closed for several hours. Many find this aspect the hardest to comprehend, but if the neglect was chronic, would it really have been that hard or would it have come naturally? She was left there perhaps _in the hope that she would never be found_, which is the clearest psychological mirror that someone thought their own neglect might be made to infect the investigation, and it did. Ultimately this case is a case characterized by neglect. A craven silence dogs this case. A sense of cool indifference from the authorities charged with prosecuting haunts it. A gnawing cowardice occupies the apologia that has developed around this case. Someone else did it, but no one knows who, so let's leave it at that. It's the pusillanimity of ignorance, and unfortunately in this world, it catches on even when what we think we're doing is paying attention.

If it took an hour to stage the note, and more hours to stage everything else, those undertaking the staging were so preoccupied with getting their story straight they utterly neglected to even notice the bow in JonBenét's hair. The neglect of the bow is mirrored in neglecting to put the right-sized panties on JonBenét as well.[54]

Think about the effort involved to put John Andrew's suitcase in place, to set up the window scene, to apply the duct tape,[55] to change JonBenét's clothes, wipe her down, wrap her in a blanket and stow her in the wine cellar – all while forgetting[56] about the bow in her hair.

But it's not only those involved in the staging that the *Christmas Star* both hides and illuminates in the darkness. No one has explicitly mentioned the bow in JonBenét's hair until this narrative, until right now. It's not explicitly mentioned in the autopsy report by the coroner either, until the section:

REMAINDER OF THE EXTERNAL EXAMINATION:[57]

*The scalp is covered by long blonde hair which is fixed in two ponytails, one on top of the head **secured by a cloth hair tie**[58] and blue elastic band, and one in the lower back of the head secured by a blue elastic band. **No scalp trauma is identified.** The external auditory canals are patent and free of blood. The eyes are green and the pupils equally dilated.*

The bow, identified as a "cloth hair tie" without giving away the colors [making it easy to miss] fooled the coroner, at least initially, who determined little more than the blonde haired scalp of a little girl. And thanks to the pageantry of the bow and two ponytails, the coroner missed any signs of trauma to the scalp, let alone the skull. Had the coroner stopped here, the murder weapon would likely have been an obvious culprit – the garrotte.

It took the coroner an extensive study of JonBenét's symmetrical chest, prepubescent breasts, abdomen and extremities, genitals, and then an internal exam through body cavities starting with the lungs, heart, spleen, adrenals, kidney, liver, pancreas and bladder before he cycled back to the skull and brain…

Upon reflection…there is found to be an extensive area of scalp hae-morrhage…This fracture measures approximately 8.5 inches in length. [But] only very minimal contusion is present…

So even the coroner was initially blinded by the *Christmas Star*. The last known photo of JonBenét alive tells us almost all we need to know about this case. On the one hand, as we've seen, it's an image of a child very different from the images we know so well of America's princess, of the child beauty queen. If this JonBenét seems to be a shadow of that JonBenét, then in the same way the cold and dead JonBenét with yellow mucous and saliva on her cheek is a shadow of the living JonBenét. They're both the same and yet *not*, just as the *Christmas Star* and the jagged tree hidden beneath it go together, and yet they don't compete equally for our attention. They're not *quite* the same thing.

If the pair the Grand Jury voted to indict for child abuse resulting in death and for being accessories to murder staged a scene to protect a child, **weren't they also trying to protect themselves?**

The accessories aspect is about one thing, but c'mon, if we're talking about staging a crime scene, that isn't about child abuse resulting in death. That's not what the abuse accusation is angling at, is it? It's about something that predated and perhaps precipitated the crime.

The question is when it turned out JonBenét was dead, did it dawn on anyone – besides her murderer – that *they might be in trouble too*? Was it a case that the Ramseys might finally be seen for who they really were [because of what had happened] and so, something extreme had to be done to make sure that didn't happen, to make sure that never happened?

Did it dawn on them that they ought to have known or done some things, several things perhaps, to protect JonBenét that they had ultimately not done, and wasn't it these sins that needed to be hidden from the world by the bright *Christmas Star* of the Ransom Note, the intruder theory, the Santa Claus-did-it theory, the pedophile abductor and everything else?

Child abuse is also a misleading term. It conjures up physical abuse, confrontation, yelling, bruises and screaming, where the abuse in this instance feels closer to the opposite of classical abuse: neglect. Neglect can also be in the form of carelessness, unwillingness or indifference.

There is no better exhibit for this indifference[59] than when Burke was asked to draw a picture of his family on January 8th, 1997, and he left JonBenét out of it. When Dr. Phil asked Burke as a 29-year-old if he consciously decided not to draw JonBenét, Burke responded:

"I don't really remember what was going through my head, but she was gone so I didn't draw her. [Shrugs and smirks]."

Or when he was asked on January 8th, 1997, how he was dealing with JonBenét's death. Burke replied:

"I don't know, I kinda forget about it 'cause I'm just [mimics playing computer game noises]."

And when darkness falls after Christmas, and the icy cold moves in we wonder: can one conjure a star back out of the darkness once its light has disappeared? How does one *make* a twinkling star of a void?

The shimmering, wheeling Christmas cosmos disappears behind a blanket of cloud and snow. A waning gibbous moon peeks between fluffy clouds, occasionally dusting the frosty streets of Boulder in silver flakes of snow, like so many sequin stars.

About the Author

Nick van der Leek [_True Crime Rocket Science_ on YouTube, _True Crime Rocket Science_ on Facebook, _@CrimeRocket_ on Twitter and _@Nickvdk_ on Instagram] is a widely published photojournalist and the author of over 95 books, including several trilogies dedicated to unravelling the world famous, and still officially unsolved JonBenét Ramsey and Madeleine McCann cases.

Instead of journalism, Van der Leek studied law, economics and marketing. After two years cutting his teeth in a busy newsroom he became a full-time investigative writer. Today he is one of the most prolific true crime authors in the world.

He has sat in on many high-profile court cases, including Oscar Pistorius, Henri van Breda and Jason Rohde, and has occasionally advised criminal prosecutors during court cases on an extemporary basis. His research on the mysterious death of Vincent van Gogh has been added to the archives of the Van Gogh Library, in Nuenen, the Netherlands.

The next Rocket Science title, SILVER FOX II, reveals additional insights into the fascinating Chris Watts case. Available early 2020.

For more information on new releases, reviews, blogs and discussions, visit crimerocket.com.

[1] The link to this interview transcript has since been scrubbed online. However a partial transcript is available here. Note this transcript doesn't contain the clip referenced above.

[2] The Ramsey's had participated in a media blitz starting on March 17th, and ending around ten days later. This blitz included appearances on Barbara Walters [CBS], ABC News, several appearances of the Today Show, Larry King [CNN] and Burden of Proof. Towards the end of this period Boulder DA Alex Hunter also appeared on the Today Show and Larry King Live On March 20th, an article appeared in Newsweek, trumpeting Smit's Intruder Theory. It was on the Barbara Walters show that the Ramseys were asked by Walters why they didn't take a lie detector test.

WALTERS: *Why didn't you take a lie detector test?*

PATSY: *No one ever asked us...*

WALTERS: *Really?*

PATSY:...*to take a lie detector test.*

WALTERS [Incredulous]: *Police never asked you to take a lie detector test?*

JOHN: *No.*

PATSY: *No.*

WALTERS: *Mr. Ramsey, would you now take a lie-detector test—*

JOHN: *I would, certainly.*

WALTERS *Would you, Mrs. Ramsey?*

PATSY: *Yes, I would take a lie-detector test.*

[3] From the Washington Post:

JonBenét Ramsey's parents no longer are willing to take a lie detector test about the 6-year-old's death because their lawyer and Boulder police cannot agree on an independent examiner to administer the exam.

"Obviously, we're disappointed that the Ramseys have declined to take the polygraph exams after very publicly saying they would," Police Chief Mark Beckner said in a statement [on the] informal deadline he set for the Ramseys to take the test. Last month, John and Patsy Ramsey told ABC's Barbara Walters.. that they would submit to an exam if the results were publicized, if it were administered independent of the Boulder police and if it were conducted in their new home town of Atlanta. Ramsey attorney Lin Wood argued that Beckner's

proposal to have the FBI conduct the test was unfair because the FBI helped investigate JonBenét's death.

[4] The first polygraph test was conducted by Jerry Toriello, a New Jersey-based polygrapher. The second polygraph [which the Ramseys passed] was conducted by Edward Gelb.

[5] Following the outcome of the polygraph test, <u>Patsy called on Boulder Police Chief Beckner to stop playing games, and tell them what to do next</u>. Beckner's response? "Come in and talk to us…We still have questions…we would like some answers…and [the Ramseys] <u>are still under the umbrella of suspicion</u>…"

[6] The *PBWorks* editor <u>intentionally provides an inaccurate name for the author of *The Craven Silence* as Nick van der Beek</u>. Although I contacted the host directly to correct this error, she ignored the request to make a correction, and despite frequent editing of the site, has refused to correct this particular error [it's not an error but a misrepresentation] for some years now.

[7] Included in the list of 76 books is *The Craven Silence* trilogy. However the seven other Rocket Science books are not included. In September 2018 the *Denver Post* acknowledged that "no fewer than 37 books have been written about the Ramsey case."

[8] Easy to miss [and perhaps intentionally] the legal aspects of CBS' the *Case of: JonBenét Ramsey* Wiki page are buried within the section titled: <u>The Ramseys</u>. The section concludes by referring to the defamation suits as "retired" rather than settled. While the section is explicit about defamation, and Lin Wood's threats, it's less explicit about how the $1 billion in suits were ultimately settled. The fact that the two-part series is still available appears to show the suit was settled in *CBS's* favor, otherwise why else would *CBS* still be allowed to broadcast them? Once again, this episode in legal chicanery fits the pageantry and legal posturing surrounding the Ramsey case perfectly.

[9] If there was [and remains] a strategy to frustrate the investigation and prosecution of the murder of JonBenét Ramsey, it has succeeded for the past 23 years and counting.

[10] The precise description of the Vagina Mucosa in the autopsy is cited by the *Denver Post* as follows:

All of the sections contain vascular congestion and focal interstitial chronic inflammation. The smallest piece of tissue, from the 7:00 position of the vaginal wall/hymen, contains epithelial erosion with underlying capillary congestion. A small number of red blood cells is present on the eroded surface, as is birefringent foreign material. Acute inflammatory infiltrate is not seen.

The birefringent material is commonly regarded as a wood fragment from the paintbrush.

[11] *"The person I see doing this is a very vicious, brutal criminal, perhaps a sadistic pedophile."* – Lou Smit on Larry King Live, May 28th, 2001

[12] Burke Ramsey's first nanny, Shirley Brady, described JonBenét's older brother as both "highly motivated" and "intelligent." According to Brady Burke "figured out at five months in his walker, how to unscrew every doorknob in his kitchen…"

[13] The exact date for the move to Boulder from Atlanta was November 21st, 1991.

[14] Patsy was diagnosed with cancer in June 1993.

[15] Source: *JonBenét: Inside the Ramsey Murder Investigation* by Steve Thomas.

[16] On December 23rd, the day following JonBenét's final pageant, a 911 call was made from the Ramsey residence during a private Christmas party. The events surrounding this emergency call remain unexplained.

[17] On February 20th, 1997 the *Daily Camera* cited Dr. Joan Slook, a paediatrician at the Baylor College of Medicine in Houston, regarding her opinion on JonBenét's medical records.

Beuf refused to comment on the case Wednesday. But Slook said: "Poor hygiene can cause chronic inflammation. Some little girls don't wash themselves properly. **Improper wiping or washing in the vaginal area** *can introduce bacteria and produce inflammation. Some little girls can have asymptomatic bladder infections that can cause irritation in the vagina. Chronic inflammation is a pretty non-specific thing to say," she said, adding that epithelial erosion also is vague.*

Here Slook seems to be referring to a little girl improperly wiping herself, but why couldn't it be a little boy?

…Slook expressed amazement at reports that JonBenét visited Beuf 30 times in the past three years, as Beuf told a television reporter Friday. "Thirty times?

That's a whole lot. I have a healthy 6-year-old daughter; she's probably been three times in the last year."

Based on Dr. Slook's measure of her own daughter, JonBenét was <u>ten times more sickly</u> than a healthy child of the same age.

[18] John Ramsey's secretary at the time was Laurie Wagner. Wagner went on to become the Vice President of the company after Ramsey departed, in fact <u>as early as September 27th, 1996</u>, an impressive career trajectory from secretary.

[19] John Ramsey was voted Boulder's Entrepreneur of the Year by the local Chamber of Commerce the following year, in 1996.

[20] When Cabell asked the Ramseys on *CNN*, on January 1st 1997 if the Ramseys would sit down and talk to the police, they were both adamant they would. Whatever the police wanted to know, they'd co-operate. Well, they wasted no time in assembling a Dream Team of lawyers, private detectives, getting an FBI Profiler to give them a clean bill of health, and assemble a PR team. Meanwhile, they wasted four months of investigative time before they did – finally – talk to the cops. When this finally happened it was under several conditions, and with their lawyers present in the room with them.

[21] In *The Craven Silence* series <u>the importance of Christmas gifts was stressed, and in particular – bicycles</u>. It was also emphasized that Burke <u>didn't get a bicycle for Christmas</u>, whereas JonBenét did. In his first ever interview, Burke went onto Dr. Phil and said, <u>"We both got bikes."</u> This assertion, however, is not supported by what both his parents said in their respective statements. From John Ramsey's Interview with police in 1998:

SMIT: *Okay. Did you go to the Barnhill's to pick up a bike?*

JOHN: *Yeah, Christmas Eve. We'd given JonBenét a bike; we got Patsy a bike. We were giving Burke a bike **but not that year.***

Any guesses what <u>the very last thing JonBenét did on Christmas Day</u>, before the sun set – for her, for the last time – and before they went to the Whites?

From *#Shakedown*:

JOHN: *JonBenét rode her bike for a moment outside before we went to the Whites; just round the patio. I'm sure that went back in the garage. Patsy's bike, I don't know, it could have gone in the garage. I don't remember.*

SMIT: *Have you seen it since, Patsy's bike?*

JOHN: *Yeah. We have it.*

SMIT: *[INAUDIBLE] took it?*

JOHN: *No.* **We gave, JonBenét's [new] bike, we gave away.**

[22] On December 23rd, 1992 the Ramseys bought a 1,731 square foot house in Charlevoix, Michigan for $336,400.

[23] The subject of bedwetting is brought up again in the chapter *Being Beautiful in the 21st Century.*

[24] The reference to the nanny by Wilcox might be to Shirley Brady or Su-zanne Savage. When Tom Trujillo interviewed Patsy on April 30th, 1997 [her first interview], he asked Patsy about bedwetting.

TRUJILO: *Do you remember back in '94, typical doctor's visit, you [filled] out all those forms, making some sort of a notation, on one of Dr. Beuf's forms about bedwetting and soiling. That was kind of a concern; [do] you remember anything?*

PATSY: *No...I was having chemotherapy. I don't remember. Suzanne took them to the doctor a lot then. My housekeeper, a nanny sort of. I don't remember. I mean if...*

This may be Patsy passing the bedwetting buck to the nannies [which she was doing in actuality as well], but whichever way you slice it, whether Patsy was justified or not because of cancer, someone else was in charge of the care of her children. Not her. Patsy not being able to remember bedwetting issues may be Patsy being economical with the truth, but it might also be partially true – in the sense that it wasn't an issue, and she didn't care, just as Jacques I and II had to sort themselves out or be done away with.

[25] When John Ramsey appeared on *CNN*, he said, referring to looking into Burke's room for JonBenét after reading the note: "We went to check our son's room, sometimes she sleeps in there." Did JonBenét sleep in Burke's bed on Christmas Eve? And did she expect to sleep there again on Christmas Night? Did she have a choice where she slept if she'd already wet her bed previously?

[26] The word attaché has been highlighted as a very unusual word for kid-nappers, foreign or domestic, to use. The link between the macron in *attaché*

and the macron in the highly unusual portmanteau of *JonBenét* cannot be overstated.

[27] Another discrepancy between the *CNN* interview in early 1997 and 2000 was in 2000 the Ramseys claimed they called the police immediately after "receiving" the note, whereas in 1997 John claimed they waited several hours for the kidnappers to call. Unbelievably, the police on hand claimed the time the kidnappers said they would call came and went without there being any explicit acknowledgement of this failure to call from the Ramseys.

[28] Bill McReynolds, who performed the role of Santa at the Ramseys' Christmas party on December 23rd, was seriously identified as a possible suspect by none other than John Ramsey himself.

JOHN [to Lou Smit]: *You know, **we were suspicious of McReynolds** I guess in the beginning and he was the only – he came to the memorial service, a good friend of mine who was there said that you guys need to go back and look at that video, because when Patsy went up to hug him, he pushed her away.*

John then suggested to Smit that a friend said McReynolds fit the profile of an elderly pedophile pretending to be feeble ["Was the feebleness an act?"] meanwhile having a keen, seditious interest in little girls.

[29] Update from Heavy.com: *In videos published on the In Memory of Katelyn Nicole Davis YouTube channel, Davis talks about fights with her mother, Tammy Rogers. The arguments range from fights over Rogers' drug use, men [such as Tammy's ex-boyfriend Anthony] who [came] over to their home and Davis cutting herself. In another video, Davis explicitly states that she has no father. Davis maintained a blog titled "**Diary of a Broken Doll.**" … Davis wrote on December 27 that she had been forced to see her stepfather. The second paragraph reads: My stepfather did a lot of things to me, that it seems I cannot forgive him for. He physically, mentally and verbally abused me. He struck me with his leather belt that has silver studs, making sure that the studs hit me. He once hit me so hard with the belt on my arm, that my arm started to bleed. He even… He tried to rape me. In another paragraph, Davis mentions two times when her stepfather told her to commit suicide. She adds, "I got into the National Leaders Association for Young Leaders. They were going to help me with college. But of course, he said I was too stupid to be in something like that, and he burned it in front of my face."*

[30] The interview with Douglas on *NBC's Dateline* was repackaged a year later and broadcast on *MSNBC's Time&Again* show in 1998.

[31] According to Douglas, H. Ellis Armistad left a message on his voice-mail indicating the Ramseys were requesting him as a defense consultant. Douglas does not indicate calling Armistad back, or when, but he had to because he alludes to telling the detective he would be in the area for several more days and was available.

[32] Douglas described his first misconception as wrongly assuming Jon-Benét was a "professional" model. Instead he was told she was simply a child participating in child beauty pageants. This is a patently ridiculous assertion given JonBenét's track record along with her mother's and aunt Pam's pageant titles. Grandma Nedra had a shrine in her Atlanta home, at the time, festooned with photos, dedicated to all the pageants her girls had won. JonBenét wasn't allowed to eat McDonalds, or get her paws dirty and Patsy was – as neighbor Joe Barnhill maintained on December 27th – "working so hard to groom her" into a child beauty queen. JonBenét could not have been a more professional child model if she'd tried!

[33] Diane Brumfitt, a school counsellor and neighbor directly to the south of the Ramsey home said she noticed the sunroom light which usually burned through the night, and had for years, didn't burn at all that night. There are various possibilities around this, one being that the Ramseys may have been aware of events sooner than later.

[34] The first lawyer John Ramsey spoke to was Mike Bynum. John asked Bynum to represent him at approximately 19:00 on December 26th, 1996. Ironically, John had just spoken in-person privately with JonBenét's paediatrician Dr. Beuf prior to hiring Bynum as counsel.

[35] In his *book Law & Disorder*, Douglas states after two hours of talking to John Ramsey he knew he was innocent.

[36] Dr. Roger Depue, a counterpart to Douglas who at one time headed the FBI's unit in charge of profiling, was requested by Dr. Bertram Brown, a psychiatrist called in by Boulder District Attorney Alex Hunter to profile the writer of the note. Depue stated, and yes, this is a quote: *"The writer is a well-educated, middle-aged female….a close relative, friend, or business associate, in that order."*

Depue also added that many aspects in the note were **ridiculous and didn't make any sense,** such as the low ransom amount, the length of the note under the circumstances, the practise note and the colloquial reference by a foreign faction to "fat cats" and "growing a brain."

Depue also highlighted a feminine tone, a familiarity with John and a nurturing personality.

"[But] the note appears to be an effort to obfuscate why [JonBenét] died." Isn't that what pageantry is – obfuscation whether by accident or design, it's the enhancement or twisting of reality to make it [and oneself] appear and feel otherwise.

[37] When Burke Ramsey was asked if he'd read the Ransom Note on the 20 year anniversary, Burke told Dr. Phil:

"I don't think I've read the whole thing; I've definitely seen pictures of it though."

[38] I like how the reporter refers to the note as so-called to an FBI Profiler who took it as genuine at face value; great gumption there.

[39] Source: The Bonita Papers.

[40] Nedra Paugh quit working for Access Graphics in 1993. It was also natural for Nedra to refer to John as Mr. Ramsey. The Bonita Papers quotes Nedra saying on one occasion: *"As long as Mr. Ramsey [brings] in the money, we'll spend it."*

[41] On May 17th, 2002 forensic handwriting examiner Gideon Epstein said the following in a deposition during Wolf vs John and Patsy Ramsey, and subsequently cited by *Fox News:*

EPSTEIN: *Chet Ubowski found there is evidence which indicates that the Ransom Note may have been written by Patsy Ramsey.*

Chet Ubowski was a forensic document examiner with the Colorado Bureau of Investigation, and also the only forensic document examiner to testify before a grand jury in the Ramsey case.

According to *Fox News:*

*"Out of 100 people [Ubowski] analyzed for the Boulder Police Department... **Ubowski found only one person whom he thought may have authored the document – Patsy Ramsey.** Investigative sources tell Fox News that*

the disguised letters and bleeding ink from the felt tipped pen used to write the note kept him from 100 percent ID of Mrs. Ramsey."

[42] When Douglas wrote a book referring to his involvement in the Ramsey case, Douglas affirmed that he saw no signs of staging by any of the Ramseys.

[43] Note the heater below the window in this rare image of Burke's room. There's also a heater in Burke's bathroom.

[44] Schuler did ask Burke where they waited on Christmas morning before their parents were awake. Burke said he was awake first – at 05:00 – and let JonBenét sleep. He said they played together in his room prior to waking up the Ramseys.

[45] It's hard to know what to make of the sack of rope. This could either be staged or something the Ramseys genuinely didn't know about. If it is staged, it suggests the guest bedroom is meant to be inferred as a possible crime scene, and if that's case it likely wasn't.

[46] "… *The garrotting and the location of her death was on the small piece of carpet located outside the wine cellar door. Her bladder let go upon death, accounting for the urine stains in the front of her clothing and carpet. The rear application of the garrotte is confirming evidence of her being on her stomach during this act."* – James Kolar via Websleuths

[47] True Crime Rocket Science agrees with Smit that the missing paint-brush piece *was* likely used to sexually assault JonBenét. This is based firstly on the discovery of a fragment of birefringent material in JonBenét's genitals, and the belief by Dr. John Meyer, the coroner, that JonBenét wasn't sexually assaulted in the conventional sense, but that she experienced "sexual contact" and was "digitally penetrated", which is quite different. Birefringent material corresponds to certain kinds of plant cellulose as well as the polymers found in paint. Both possibilities potentially match the idea of paintbrush fragment, particularly the latter.

[48] One way to camouflage one's handwriting is to use one's left hand to write if one is usually right-handed and vice versa. Ironically Patsy was am-bidextrous, so she theoretically had the option of writing with one or both hands.

[49] The final chapter in this narrative makes the case for why the children were almost certainly awake late into the night.

[50] Or worst.

[51] *"She [JonBenét] was a spark plug in our lives."* — John Ramsey to Paula Woodward

[52] John's first affair was with Gloria Williams in the late 70's. Kim Ballard was on the radar of Boulder police and interviewed by Geraldo Rivera in May 1997. Ballard claimed she put an ad in *USA Today* which led to an affair from November '94 to April '95 during Patsy's first ovarian cancer treatment and recovery.

[53] In Paula Woodward's book *We Have Your Daughter* a photo of a book is depicted. It's claimed that John Ramsey read from this book to the whole family on Christmas Eve.

[54] JonBenét was found dressed in size 12-14 panties. In addition the coroner believed JonBenét's private parts had been wiped down with a cloth.

[55] Due to the nature of fibers found on the sticky side, the duct tape was likely applied *post mortem*. The duct tape was used to impute an older, more seasoned attacker. Like the Ransom Note, the duct tape was also a form of pageantry intended to direct attention away from one impression and towards another.

[56] It's quite possible the bow was intentionally "forgotten" in the hair to conceal the injury, but this assumes those involved in the alleged cover-up knew about the injury.

[57] Source: *The Denver Post*.

[58] Linda Arndt refers to green Christmas garland in JonBenét's hair. It's not certain whether she saw actual green garland or mistook the hair bow for something else.

[59] In his book *Foreign Faction*, James Kolar refers to a comment from Burke during his interview with Dr. Bernhard seeming to him to be "extremely callous" and suggesting "little care or concern" by the nine-year-old.

NOTES

NOTES

NOTES

NOTES

NOTES

NOTES

NOTES

NOTES

CHRISTMAS

STAR

By Nick van der Leek

Cover design: Nick van der Leek

"Let justice be done though thy heavens fall."
— <u>Latin legal adage</u>

"I'd like to shake every one of the grand jurors' hands because they know this mother and father couldn't have hurt their child." — Shirley Brady, former housekeeper

"I thought JonBenét was gonna be there, I thought they found her, so I came in excited, almost relieved." — Burke Ramsey

Important Note to the Reader:

The Rocket Science books are unique. Throughout this book, the author has provided hyperlinks to relevant resources including documents, photographs and videos to enhance your interactivity with the story.

Table Of Contents